Embracing Desire

Embracing Desire

LOUIS ROY

WIPF & STOCK · Eugene, Oregon

Wipf & Stock
An Imprint of Wipf and Stock Publishers
199 W. 8th Ave., Suite 3
Eugene, OR 97401

www.wipfandstock.com

PAPERBACK ISBN: 978-1-5326-8384-8
HARDCOVER ISBN: 978-1-5326-8385-5
EBOOK ISBN: 978-1-5326-8386-2

Manufactured in the U.S.A.   MAY 13, 2019

Translated by Robert Czerny, with the assistance of Pierrot Lambert

"Let everyone who is thirsty come.
Let anyone who wishes take the water of life as a gift."

(Rev 22:17)

Contents

Acknowledgements | xi

Introduction | xiii

1   Desire Described | 1
     Layers of Desire | 1
     Needs and Desires | 5
     The Reality Principle and Finitude | 8
     The Horizon of Infinitude | 11

2   Happiness | 16
     Judaism and Happiness | 17
     Christianity and Happiness | 18
     Moral Laxity | 20
     Rigorism | 21
     A Hierarchy | 24

3   Beyond Optimism and Pessimism | 26
     On Human Potential | 27
     The Origins of Modern Optimism | 27
     Sheep and Goats | 29
     No Neutral Middle Ground | 30
     Christianity Is Hope | 32

4   THREE FORMS OF HOPE | 34
         Everyday Hope | 35
         Religious Hope | 36
         Christian Hope | 38

5   CONSECRATION OF DESIRE | 42
         The Heart Which Does Not Give Itself | 43
         An Initial Reconciliation | 44
         Acceptance of the Negative | 45
         Attachment-Detachment | 46
         Purification of Desire | 47

6   A PATH TOWARDS MYSTERY | 49
         Our Amazing Desire | 49
         Invitation to Mystery | 50
         Forms of Consciousness | 52
         Some Features of Mystical Consciousness | 52
         Rereading Cassian | 54
         Mystical Consciousness and the Everyday | 55

7   DISSATISFACTION | 56
         A Transition | 57
         Complementary Opposites | 59
         Supports | 60
         Ambiguous Witnessing | 62
         A Difficult Tension | 63

8   DESIRABILITY | 65
         Shared Energy | 65
         The Question and the Experience of God | 68
         The Awareness of Being Desirable | 71

9   LIBERATION OF DESIRE | 73
       Two Forms of Guilt | 74
       Sin as a Failure of Desire | 77
       The Freedom that Jesus Offers | 80

10   SPIRITUAL ACCOMPANIMENT | 85
       Love and Desire | 85
       Ambivalence and Guilt | 87
       Recognizing Sin | 89
       Inner Division | 91
       Welcoming the Resurrection | 92
       Conclusion | 95

Select Bibliography | 97

Acknowledgements

THE MAIN SOURCE OF inspiration of my book *Libérer le désir* comes from an Englishman, Sebastian Moore. That book has been well received in France, in the French-speaking part of Canada, and even in Mexico. It was used in a seminar at the Dominican University College in Ottawa. For these reasons, I rejoice that it is now available for American and other English-speaking readers. I thank Robert Czerny, assisted by Pierrot Lambert, for the beautiful translation. Thanks also to Matthew Wimer, assistant managing editor at Wipf & Stock, for the invaluable guidance he provided during the editorial process leading to the publication of this book. And I admire the perseverance of Anne Louise Mahoney and Pierre LaViolette who, along with Wipf & Stock's copyeditors, readied the original manuscript for printing.

Where adequate English translations of quoted passages originally in other languages are available, these have been used and footnoted accordingly. In some cases, excerpts are from online texts that lack page numbers.

The spelling is British, because all three of us are Canadians. We follow the usual guidelines of inclusive language regarding people, either by employing the plural or by alternating "he" and "she" in successive paragraphs where these pronouns are required. However, in accord with biblical language, God is referred to as "he." The very few biblical quotations are from the New Revised Standard Version, in *The New Oxford Annotated Bible*. Throughout this volume, unless otherwise indicated, italicization is by the authors themselves.

Introduction

WHERE DOES DESIRE LEAD? The very question bespeaks uncertainty and ambivalence about desire: a human dynamism that is both indispensable and treacherous. On the one hand, we fear that it will take us too far and into excess that could be our downfall; on the other hand, we fear that it will play us false and disappoint us so greatly as to leave us lifeless. Should we then be wary of our desire, either because of its strength or because of its weaknesses? And yet we remain enthralled by the possibilities that desire lays before us.

Desire is essential to us as human beings. Unfortunately, we do not explore our desire fully. Moreover, we harbour a great number of desires, and the choices we make do not always coincide with our thirst for happiness.

But what in fact is desire? In the modern Western world, two schools of thought provide interpretations—one negative, the other positive. According to the first, desire is rooted in the experience of a lack, and therefore of suffering. For the second, desire begins with the stirrings of an abundance of life, and therefore of appetite for life. The first defines desire as the urge to have needs fulfilled; the second defines it as the will to live and the wish to continue to enjoy life. The first camp includes Descartes, Hobbes, Locke, Sartre, and most psychoanalysts; the second counts Spinoza, Schopenhauer, Nietzsche, and Sebastian Moore (of whom we will speak later). I favour the second group, though I accept some insights from the first (as we shall see). In fact, I will attempt to develop a third position that I hope will be more complete than the other two.

This third perspective has its origins in Plato, and it became widespread in Ancient Greece and the Latin Middle Ages. In Plato's dialogue *The Symposium*, Socrates reminds us that Eros is the son of *Penia* (Poverty) and of *Poros* (Wealth). Eros is a creator who is both poor because of his state of privation and rich because he is capable of producing many forms of beauty. The highly evocative Eros myth suggests a path of inquiry. We could follow it by saying that, since Freud, sexuality is both a source of deep dissatisfaction and a creative force. Freud was not wrong to think that sexual desire is the same as desire as such, because the latter seeks union and this union is represented by sexual fantasies. This does not prevent desire from sublimating—or, better, from being spiritualized—by focussing on the interpersonal relationship. But the sexual aspects are still present even when genitality is secondary.

Then we have René Girard's well-known and justifiably admired theses on desire. Unfortunately, his concept of desire is as restricted as that of Thomas Hobbes. It depicts desire as essentially mimetic and competitive, leading inevitably to violence. This is desire-as-need, accompanied by envy. Girard's analyses on this topic are enlightening.[1] However, my work will explore a form of desire that is much more profound and humanizing, which Girard does not address.

The purpose of this book is to provide signposts to help us to distinguish the many types of desire and to emphasize those that are most rewarding and therefore merit our committed and even total involvement. This is my main message: contrary to what many Christians and many psychoanalysts have said, the wise approach is not to diminish desire but to intensify it. This amounts to nothing less than desiring one's desire.

Here is how we shall proceed. I will begin by describing four types of desire and how they interact, while also showing how much the finitude and infinitude of desire are linked inextricably in a rich, full human life. We will next see that Christianity values

---

1. For a brief discussion of Girard see Roy, "Why is the Death?" 129–39.

happiness. We will then ask how Christian hope can reach out beyond optimism and pessimism and can account for ordinary hope and religious hope. We will explore further questions: Can our desire be consecrated, and can it become a path into Mystery? We will also stress the complementarity between dissatisfaction and fullness. We will conclude with three chapters on what I have learned from Sebastian Moore regarding the desirability of a person, the freeing of desire, and the consequences of this liberation for spiritual counselling.

I am sharing these thoughts in the hopes of suggesting paths for further research and advancing the boundaries of the subject. I will cite the Bible and a large number of authors, psychoanalysts, philosophers, and theologians, but I will express my thoughts in a direct manner most of the time without engaging in erudite declamation. Though based mostly on my personal reflections, this book took shape in dialogue with contemporary thinkers and with others who attended my courses and lectures.

I

Desire Described

I WILL PRESENT FOUR types of desire in this chapter and describe how they interact. I will then apply the reality principle and its link to finitude to the field of desire. I will end by sketching the role of what I refer to as a horizon of infinitude.

Layers of Desire

Desire has so many forms that one ought to speak of "desires." Let us consider the four layers[1] of desire. The *first layer* comprises physiological needs: eating, drinking, sexual pleasure, and a feeling of well-being in one's body (visceral, nervous, muscular, tactile). Physical objects are necessary to satisfy these needs: food, drink, bodily presence, temperature, as well as a wide range of chemical and biological conditions. Many different things come into play, such as utensils, tools, appliances, houses, buildings, and water, electrical, and heating services—all of which are supported by vast social, economic, and political systems. In this domain of everyday

1. The author's terms are *paliers* of desire, collectively in an étagement; these words denote floors or landings and storeys in buildings. We have translated *paliers* as *layers*. But other terms would do equally well: for instance, forms, manifestations, types, levels, or stages of desire. (Translator's note)

living and its required organization, where *material* goods are the issue, I suggest that it is better to speak of needs than desires. We will see why presently.

The *second layer* deals with desires properly speaking: desires that have to do with *cultural* goods such as the meaning to be found in human relationships, at work, and in recreation, sport, the arts, and intellectual pursuits. What turns a quite small number of brute needs into innumerable desires is the application of *meaning* to needs. Although the kinds of products that we consume are very familiar, it is the way they are constantly being packaged that gives rise to their great diversity and helps us to avoid boredom. Needs are accompanied by fantasies arising from drives and affects, whereas desires come to the fore in the presence of meanings linked to symbols. Clearly, needs are subsumed by desires in the course of being cultivated, or, better, "culture-ated," and most of the time this occurs without conscious reflection. Thus, humans sharing a meal is more than the intake of nourishment by animals, and likewise sport is more than a series of physical exercises. As the philosopher Jean Granier has noted, whereas material goods are quantitative in nature, cultural goods offer limitless possibilities and variations because they are qualitative.[2]

Going further, eros between individuals is more than sexuality in the sense of genitality—arts of conversation, of closeness, of contact belong to it. So here we reach the third layer in the scale of desires, above material and cultural goods. Here, the person as such comes into play. Indeed, she is her own object of desire, aspires to be a value for herself, and affirms herself as such. And this cannot be achieved without others, since an individual cannot acquire identity and value independently of others. Thus, we observe here a desire for the other that goes beyond what another can bring us in terms of material and cultural goods. The self seeks recognition from the other: recognition of its individual, unique, and irreplaceable value; recognition accompanied by signs that the other person is truly attracted to me, that is to say, loves me.

2. See Granier, *Le désir du moi*, 100–101; I found chapters 4 and 5 particularly helpful.

The self is moved when it perceives desire on the part of the other, that it is desired by the other. As many authors have noted, the self is then touched by a desire for the desire that the other feels. Should one ask for love, the request is satisfied when the other manifests her desire, rather than professing her esteem (even if well-deserved) or offering a special gift.

It is clear that desire among humans presupposes receptivity, which means accepting a gift from those who show an interest in us. Recognition then arrives from outside oneself. And yet, some people manage to interiorize this recognition, thereby allowing for a kind of self-esteem that does not depend upon constant reinforcement from others. For these fortunate individuals, a solid autonomy evolves progressively, as fantasies arising from drives and affects vanish to the extent that they transmute into a web of fertile symbols. The psychoanalyst Françoise Dolto points out that desire is rich in language and communication when it transcends immediate satisfaction:

> *The love relationship is never linked to immediate satisfaction in response to the express demands of the child.* In fact, both the call and search for the other cease when desire is satisfied, and the invention of ways to convey them ceases too. Satisfaction of desire puts a stop to the call. And when the call ends, the tension of desire also disappears, and so does love. The pleasurable aspects may still be enjoyed, but if this enjoyment is not enveloped in language—that is, if it is not yet symbolized through the modulations of exchanges with the other, be it by gesture and imitation or in more or less articulate verbalization— then what remains for a subject who has been satisfied too rapidly bears no useable marker by which memory may retain a representation of the drive of this desire. When tension disappears too quickly, neither the desire nor the enjoyment is experienced as "poetic," that is, creative. In the absence of exchanges between people and of words to allow the imagination to share the pleasure that comes with communication, the rapid satisfaction of a desire once again causes the child to confuse the fulfilled

> desire with the need from which, in its primordial origin,
> that desire was indistinguishable.[3]

Language allows one to distance oneself from needs. Moreover, with language comes a capacity for a "dialoguing autonomy" in a person who seeks self-realization with another in an enlightened manner. True self-affirmation presupposes a love of self, and more precisely a love for myself who desires, a love of my desire, a desire of my desire: I desire to be a being-who-desires by affirming my integral desire, constituted by both finitude and infinitude. At the same time, I want others to be beings-who-desire towards me, and to be such in complete freedom, independently of me and with each other and with God. The demands that I make on them adjust to what they can and wish to give. As we shall see in chapter 7, the acceptance of multiple instances of dissatisfaction is an integral feature of the reality of desire. As a result, by respecting others and recognizing their freedom, I uphold their deepest desire.

The highest degree of desire, which I place at the *fourth layer*, is openness to the Infinite. Not infinite in the sense of indefinite, the unending sequence of limited occurrences—this is the "false infinite" that Hegel justifiably rejected. And not even the infinite that Hegel himself proposes, an infinite of which every finite being constitutes the Totality, with the consequence that no finite being can encounter it as Other.[4] Rather, the real, actual Infinite, pure Act, which alone brings others into being, as Thomas Aquinas saw. Later on in this chapter, we will see what sort of access to God is made possible by desire. For the time being, let us simply note that it is God's desire—the desire that God has for us—that makes us exist and that establishes our fundamental value as human beings worthy of being desired. If God takes human desire seriously, unreservedly so, it is because he himself created it. Therefore the love of oneself—which begins with the desire that parents have

3. Dolto, *Au jeu du désir*, 292–93.

4. Regarding the rejection of Hegelian Totality, see Levinas, *Totality and Infinity*. I do not agree entirely with how Levinas views the Infinite; yet he rightly saw that the Infinite can only be delineated within the relationship between one human being and another human perceived as other.

for their child, grows in continuity with many other human presences and reaches full expression in the affirmation of self—has its ultimate foundation in the creative act of God. "I am honoured in the sight of the Lord," declares the prophet Isaiah (49:5).

Needs and Desires

Consistent with what I have proposed regarding the four layers, I will distinguish four main types of desire: physiological, cultural, interpersonal, and divine. The first is need in its strict sense, which leads to death if totally unmet. The second could be referred to as artificial need, not in the negative sense but rather in its etymological guise of "made with art." There is much scope in this second type for choices, substitutions, renunciations, creations. However, both these types presuppose an initial lack that triggers a process leading to the experience of satisfying the lack.

By contrast, it would be wrong to define the third and fourth layers of desire as needs, since needs are defined as wants or lacks to be filled (à *combler*). Undeniably, a lack is experienced to the extent that the individual remains incapable of possessing the objects of his desire. But it is not a matter of a lack *to be* filled, in the sense of making the need disappear—it is not like filling a hole or an empty space, or like bringing to a close a situation where something had been missing. On these higher layers, in fact, it is neither possible nor desirable to be fully satisfied. In the novel *The Notebooks of Malte Laurids Brigge*, Malte's mother fervently advises him: "Never forget to make a wish, Malte. I don't think there is such a thing as fulfillment, but there are wishes that endure, that last a whole lifetime, so that anyhow one couldn't wait for their fulfillment."[5]

The philosopher-theologian Benoît Garceau states: "While need implies *something to be consumed*, desire implies *someone with whom to communicate*." He goes on to expand on this idea in three parts:

5. Rilke, *Notebooks*, 86–87.

(1) Contrary to need, it [desire] cannot be *satiated*. There is always an impetus in desire to go further. It is essential to desire to traverse the boundaries of its object. (2) While need is met by obtaining that which was sought, desire focuses on otherness and draws nourishment from a relationship with the other without the other ever ceasing to be other. (3) Finally, again by contrast with need, desire in its essence is non-possessive. To maintain itself and grow, it must ceaselessly renounce possessiveness.[6]

The Husserlian phenomenologist Renaud Barbaras speaks of an "original desire that is deeper than any particular lack, the scope of which surpasses and conditions the nature of its object." He explains further:

It is essential for desire that the object which satisfies it also intensifies it to the precise extent that it satisfies the desire; with the result that satisfaction of a desire implies its renewal rather than its abolition . . . Need refers back to a precise lack, it aims to restore vital wholeness, and that is why need is always need of something in particular. On the contrary, desire is not based on a lack, and in the strictest sense, it lacks nothing. The yearning that permeates it is not the opposite of absence; it surpasses vital needs, it is pure excess.[7]

Interpersonal relationships do not satisfy the desire; they deepen desire and give it new life. It would be impossible to possess entities as rich as human persons or God. As Maurice Zundel affirms, God is "the Non-possessible Value," for he is also and firstly "the Non-possessing."[8] Rather than deploring the fact that total satisfaction is unattainable, we should rejoice over it, for it testifies to a wonderful possibility: that of joyfully loving someone inexhaustible. In fact, God alone is inexhaustible, although others can also be so in their own way, derivatively, as it were—by receiving their

---

6. Garceau, *La voie du désir*, 13.

7. Barbaras, *Le désir*, 136.

8. Zundel, *Morale et mystique*, 136–37.

attractiveness from God and leading to God in the manner of fruitful and richly appreciated stepping stones.

To the extent that we find it acceptable not to be fulfilled, we enjoy the inexhaustible wealth that our daily lives offer us. We savour the presence of others as other in their otherness, which is both fascinating and challenging. This is a challenge that *material* goods could not pose: inevitably we possess them, absorb them, consume them—all these conditions are possible because of their weak otherness—and easily transform their status as other into the state of being identical with ourselves.

Moreover, *cultural* goods are ambiguous in this respect. In a centripetal or egocentric fashion, we can assimilate them to ourselves, in both senses of the word "assimilate"—considering them to be utterly similar to us, and making them fully our own. On the other hand, in centrifugal fashion, we can allow them to put us off balance and expose us to the strangely different reality that they represent. In the first case, we become slaves to the parade of our greedy choices, which always leave us disappointed. In the second case, the brilliance of all great art and literature is to unleash our hidden desire—they can even propel it, force it into the open!—by presenting aspects of reality that we ignore most of the time. This gives us the opportunity to avoid simply flitting about in all directions, and to delve deeply into what is worthwhile in order to find the extraordinary in the everyday.

The Reality Principle and Finitude

Sigmund Freud, the founder of psychoanalysis, distinguished between the pleasure principle, bound to what is immediate and short-term, and the reality principle that is capable of aiming at long-term results. Unfortunately, his positivistic philosophy did not allow him to acknowledge the degree to which the world open to humans surpasses what their biological aspect can explain.[9]

---

9. Roy, *Coherent Christianity*, 43–45.

Nevertheless, his distinction is very useful and I would like to apply it to the dialectic of desire.

In spite of appearances to the contrary, desire is weak and fearful in persons guided mainly by the pleasure principle. Such individuals allow themselves to be controlled by impulses and affects and by phantasms with little relation to reality. They have a fear of reality, caused by the threats, dangers, and demands of the real world. More precisely, as the psychoanalyst Melanie Klein has noted, the greedy child—and later the greedy adult—suffers from a twofold anxiety: that of being deprived of what she needs, and the more fundamental anxiety of not deserving to be loved. This insecurity transforms into a constant need for attention. "This greed," she writes, "is the mark of a domineering and insatiable desire that simultaneously surpasses what the subject needs and what the object can provide."[10] Such ridiculous and occasionally tragic greed is portrayed well in the films of Luis Bunuel, where the gap between reality and human desire is often "surrealistic."

By contrast, desire in someone attuned to the reality principle is a sign of a strong self. This desire is mature, intense, and daring. This person still calculates benefits and risks, as much out of respect for his reality as for the reality of others with whom he relates. This dual reality is set aside when satisfaction is pursued in a myopic manner. "Whereas the satisfaction of need effaces the otherness of the thing possessed, desire is not to be satisfied but to be lived, so as to constitute my personal identity through an interrelationship between myself and the other, where both are characterized by imperfection or lack."[11] This is why desire does not demand everything, and not all at once. Mature desire keeps me from demanding that the other be perfect, that the other be some sort of little god or idol capable of meeting all my expectations.

Now what might appear to be a constraint is actually an amplification of desire. Desire operates and manifests itself in space and time, which amounts to living within finitude. The American psychologist Rollo May has adopted a French saying: "The aim of

10. Klein, *Envy and Gratitude*, 180.

11. Jacques, *Différence et subjectivité*, 83.

desire is not its satisfaction but its prolongation."[12] Limitation and delay allow desire to be prolonged. But as he also says, in no way does this deny the value of the very intense loving moment, of "an ideal situation which ought to be somewhere in the relation lending meaning to the drab and dull days which also come."[13]

We have talked about greed, which Klein regards as a sickness of desire. The great writer Dostoyevsky masterfully portrayed a sinister and fateful variation, a sort of greed for freedom that becomes an irrationality of desire. Various of his characters— Jacques Madaule mentions Raskolnikov, Stavrogin, Versilov, and Ivan Karamazov—are obsessed with their freedom, understood as being able to do anything at all. They completely abandon reason in order to affirm this pure liberty. As Dostoyevsky's unnamed character declares in *Notes from Underground*:

> This can only mean that for men this obstinacy and wilfulness was in actual fact more agreeable to them than any kind of personal advantage . . . All man needs is *independent* volition, whatever that independence might cost and wherever it might lead . . . [M]an may deliberately and consciously desire something that is harmful, even stupid, even extremely stupid [in order] to *have the right* to desire what is even extremely stupid and not to be duty bound to desire only what is intelligent. You see, the height of stupidity is your caprice, gentlemen, and in fact might be more advantageous to us than anything else on earth, especially in certain circumstances. But in particular it can be more advantageous than any other advantage even when it obviously does us harm and contradicts the soundest conclusions of our reasoning about advantage, because at any rate it preserves what is most precious and most important to us, and that is our personality and our individuality.[14]

12. May, *Love and Will*, 75.

13. May, *Love and Will*, 102–103.

14. Dostoyevsky, *Notes from Underground* and *Double*, 19, 24, and 26. Even before Dostoyevsky, Edgar Allan Poe had pointed to this strange "perversity" in "Black Cat" and "Imp of the Perverse"; see Poe, *Tales*, 75–80 and 137–40.

This independence ends in self-destruction as well as the destruction of others. Madaule comments: "In effect, Dostoyevsky's most disturbing heroes are men who are free but no longer know the purpose of their freedom. Thus they are capable—almost indifferently—of the greatest crimes and the most extreme self-denial. Or better, they can carry out the one and the other simultaneously."[15]

In our times, this irrationality of desire is noticeable, for example, among certain major financiers, bankers, or presidents of multinational companies who have no regard for honesty or for the environment; or, further, at the individual level, people lost to alcoholism, gluttony, drug addiction, eroticism, gambling—Dostoyevsky's shocking description of which, in *The Gambler*, was based on his own experience. So many cases of flagrant contempt for the reality principle. Here, instead of being seen as desire's ally, the reality principle is shunned as a constraint on desire that is regarded as free but in fact is merely arbitrary.

Another flawed tendency, superficially opposed to greed but actually able to be its partner, consists in avoiding any sincere, firm commitment in interpersonal relationships. A restrictive understanding of "reality" allows desire to protect itself against being disappointed by others. It concentrates on material and cultural goods, forgetting the marvellous possibilities that human relationships offer. How paradoxical it seems that a lively interest in material and cultural goods can co-exist in an individual with a resigned or apathetic attitude in the interpersonal sphere. The imagination engages without restraint in the first sphere but is suppressed in the second.

I find it astonishing that many psychoanalysts—certainly Freud[16] and Lacan[17]—expect very little from interpersonal love and nothing at all from divine love. They put excessive emphasis

15. Madaule, *Dostoïevski*, 116.

16. Freud, *Civilization*; see chapter 3 regarding the third source of human suffering.

17. Lacan, *Seminar*. Fundamental desire always remains oriented towards the mother, who is simultaneously the longed-for object in incest and the great taboo; accordingly, it is impossible to satisfy desire.

on human finitude while denying the infinitude that accompanies it.[18] Dostoyevsky gives a striking account of this reduction of desire when his Grand Inquisitor proposes an institutionalized and condescending religion that would relieve humans of a freedom that they find burdensome.[19]

The Horizon of Infinitude

Some believe that an unrestrained emphasis on human finitude is a way to avoid suffering. We separate interpersonal love from divine love; we try to live the first without the resources that flow from the second. Deprived of these religious resources, the finitude that we encounter in ourselves and others can diminish hope. Can we imagine that without a horizon of infinitude, it will remain possible for us to preserve a vigorous hopefulness and to practise effective forgiveness? I write "horizon of infinitude" rather than "presence of God" so as to recognize the achievements in this difficult domain of those who call themselves agnostics or humanists, yet in whose work a horizon of infinitude can actually be detected, exercising an unspoken influence.[20]

The writings of the Anglican apologist C. S. Lewis give an idea of the sort of desire that accompanies a feeling of infinitude. Lewis adopts an expression from Wordsworth, "surprised by joy," for the title of his account of his first three decades. Lewis describes this strange joy as something "bittersweet" that suddenly came upon him several times, only to lose it afterwards and remember it with longing.[21] How to define it: as an "intense desire," "an unsatisfied

18. By contrast, in his *Wings of Desire*, "Wim Wenders has filmed the story of a dual desire: the human in search of the infinite and of the lightness of angels, and the angel in search of the finitude and weight of the human." Causse, "La défroque," 557–71.

19. Dostoyevsky, *Brothers Karamazov*, part II, book V, chapter 5.

20. Regarding finitude and infinitude in human beings see Roy, *Transcendent Experiences*, particularly chapters 5 and 9 and Conclusion. See also Roy, "Clarifying Note," 51–56.

21. Lewis, *Surprised by Joy*, 23–24, 74, 158, and 224, and Lewis, *Pilgrim's Regress*, 7 and 10.

desire which is itself more desirable than any other satisfaction";
as "a particular kind of unhappiness or grief." Its features are "the
stab, the pang, the inconsolable longing." Paradoxically, this mere
wanting is experienced as a sort of delight, a desire that continues
to be treasured even when there is absolutely no hope of its ever
being satisfied. In truth, "the very nature of Joy makes nonsense of
our common distinction between having and wanting. There, to
have is to want and to want is to have." So fruition has no part of
desire, because the human soul is so constituted as to revel in what
it can never have—what cannot even be imagined to be given—
within the bounds of real experience in our spatiotemporal world.

Another writer in the same vein is François Cheng, a French
author of Chinese origin. Here he writes about one of his characters, Dao-sheng, who is suffering because the absence of his
beloved Lan-ying has left a hole in his heart:

> Little by little, the hole filled up with something that he
> could not describe. That he scarcely tried to identify.
> Some mixture of regret, of longing, of acceptance, and
> perhaps even—strange as it might seem—of "happiness."
> Yes, happiness; to be sure, not a happily contented feel-
> ing; rather a kind of sad recognition that had been sensed
> many times already and now was affirmed with certainty.
> Recognition of what had happened [the life that the two
> lovers had shared].

The author comments:

> Is not the fulfillment of desire located within the desire
> itself? In any case, for better or for worse, Dao-sheng gave
> himself over to this idea, knowing clearly that he could
> not escape it. Everything else was trivial and meaningless
> to him. By degrees, increasingly, he pondered the mysti-
> cal passion that lived inside him and at the same time lay
> ahead of him.

And further:

> He turned with fervent resolve to a new phase, a time
> when spontaneous vitality and fulfilled desire, renewed
> hope and the end of waiting were reconciled. All his

anxieties had calmed, all terrors vanquished, so he was able to devote himself to monkish tasks with both exemplary regularity and a unique spirit of detachment.[22]

These descriptions of desire by Lewis and Cheng give a very good idea of the fundamental dynamism of mystical life, to which we will return in chapter 6. We are certainly not dealing here with a deficiency to be corrected or made whole, as if filling a void. To this point Emmanuel Levinas writes: "True Desire is that which the Desired does not satisfy but deepens. It is goodness."[23]

Elsewhere Levinas states:

> The negativity of the *In-* of the Infinite—otherwise than being, divine comedy—hollows out a desire that could not be filled, one nourished from its own increase, exalted as Desire—one that withdraws from its satisfaction as it draws near to the Desirable. This is a Desire for what is beyond satisfaction, which does not identify, as need does, a term or an end.

He adds: "Affected by the Infinite, Desire cannot go to an end to which it might be equal; in Desire, the approach creates distance [éloigne], and enjoyment is only the increase of hunger."[24]

When Cheng speaks of "satisfied desire," he does not think of it as a desire that ends but as a fullness coupled with a great nostalgia. Desire's joy is thus found outside of the incompatibility between happiness and unhappiness, between grief and joy. Fully embraced, this bittersweet feeling provokes a detachment in us that simultaneously demotes and elevates all of the less lofty forms of desire. This basic feeling, which mystics consider to be

22. Cheng, *L'éternité*, 274, 275–76, and 277. The translation here differs from that of the book's English version, *Green Mountain, White Cloud*, trans. Timothy Bent (New York: St. Martin's, 2004). The claim that the fulfilment of desire occurs within desire itself also appears in another of his splendid novels, *Le Dit de Tianyi*, 96 and 132.

23. Levinas, *En découvrant*, 175.

24. Levinas, *Of God*, 67–68. I do not believe that these lines contradict what Aristotle and Thomas Aquinas wrote about the ultimate end, given that, according to them, it can never be attained on earth.

permanent, allows both the finitude and the infinitude of desire to be embraced unreservedly in everyday reality.

Thus it is legitimate to find no contradiction between two apparently opposed affirmations of the Bible. On the one hand, Wisdom proclaims: "Those who eat of me will hunger for more, and those who drink of me will thirst for more" (Sir 24:21). On the other hand, Jesus declares: "Whoever comes to me will never be hungry, and whoever believes in me will never be thirsty" (John 6:35; see also John 4:14).

An illuminating distinction can be made between fulfilment and fullness. The hope to reach fullness is naïve because it does not take the reality principle into account. Those who seek fullness employ various strategies—ever more possessions, proliferation of pleasures, variety of experiences. But all this cannot stave off a feeling of pointless repetition. The error here is to stake one's desire totally on a goal that is infinite in appearance alone—an idol that is frequently associated (at least implicitly) with some type of Mother Goddess whose magical power eradicates all need and anxiety, all questions and doubt, every thrust towards an uncertain future. This state of the soul is illusory because it denies human finitude. Instead, it yearns to merge with some Totality—whether it is unitary (God, the cosmos) or plural—that produces a global euphoria by means of multiple different stimuli.

By contrast, fullness is experienced like a sort of peace within incompleteness. This fullness is the product of the presence-absence of an Infinite—an Infinite revealed simultaneously as wanting to share its life and, nevertheless, as other. This constitutes a mystical participation (presence) built on an ontological difference (absence). Such absence makes God distinct from all beings that are purely present; and it makes God so much more compelling because the absence shows itself at the same time to be a unique presence. It follows that desire for this absent God may gain intensity from the very fact of this absence at the same time as it produces a profound joy. Fullness-incompleteness is an eschatological anticipation, the biblical hope for a better future "ad-vent" given by the Lord of history.

In conclusion, the wise attitude towards desire consists in accepting its four types: physiological, cultural, interpersonal, and divine. The point is not to oppose them to one another or to do away with the lower forms, but to respect their hierarchy. Then the acquisition of material goods will be guided by personal priorities for cultural goods, reflecting the sort of person that one is. Cultural goods in turn will serve a sharing among friends that leads to communion rooted in the great values. Finally, divine presence will establish an incomparable peace that both modulates and encourages the pursuit of limited goals as mediating steps towards the Infinite. "A man is never happy till his vague striving has itself marked out its proper limitation."[25]

---

25. Jarno, in Goethe, *Wilhelm.*

2

Happiness

> Saint-Just said that happiness is a new idea in Europe.
> It would be easy to contest the claim and show that the
> desire for happiness has been extremely profound and
> constant throughout human history . . . But this would
> be to misunderstand Saint-Just. What his thinking sug-
> gests as a new idea is happiness for all.[1]

SAINT-JUST WAS A FRENCH revolutionary, a writer and politically engaged—and with Robespierre, tasted the "happiness for all" of the guillotine in 1794! His famous affirmation, issued towards the end of the eighteenth century, provides a good summary of Enlightenment philosophy. Thanks to the growth and application of scientific method in the seventeenth century, technological development had brought about more sustained material progress than in previous times. As shown by Dutch and Flemish paintings of the era, life was improving for the bourgeoisie; were it not for war and industrial exploitation, the misery of the working masses would have begun to lessen well before the twentieth century.

So we can readily understand that the eighteenth-century hope of happiness for all was "a new idea in Europe." Towards the

1. Lacroix, *Le désir*, 7.

end of the following century, this idea was reinforced by other factors, such as the growth of political democracy, wider access to education, and the beginnings of social measures in aid of the poor. In our times, thanks to the prosperity that followed World War II, communications media have succeeded in spreading the belief in happiness. In this context, psychology in North America—which is fundamentally optimistic, contrary to European psychoanalysis—presents practical exercises for achieving self-fulfilment and personal growth.[2]

Various thinkers have characterized our culture in different ways: Hans Selye defends altruistic egoism,[3] Philip Rieff critiques the abuse of the therapeutic model,[4] Christopher Lasch attacks it for its narcissism,[5] while Daniel Yankelovich sees a world in which material resources are becoming less abundant.[6] Despite the differences, our culture remains a culture—even a cult—of happiness. The search for happiness takes the beguiling form of a pursuit of pleasure, which is abetted by the huge variety of pleasant activities we find on offer.

Judaism and Happiness

To understand how Christianity tries to meet the novel challenge it faces in the culture of happiness, we need to recall some of the earlier ways in which it dealt with happiness. And since the roots of Christianity are in Judaism, let us begin there.

Happiness is not the principal idea of the Hebrew Bible; nevertheless, the importance of happiness is underscored in its pages. What is more dominant is the idea of election, covenant, and promise by God in favour of Israel. In this context, human happiness follows from the blessing of Yahweh, by which he wishes,

2. Some thoughts on psychologism are offered in Roy, *Coherent Christianity*, 52–54 and 91–92.

3. Selye, *Stress without Distress*.

4. Rieff, *Triumph of the Therapeutic*.

5. Lasch, *Culture of Narcissism*.

6. Yankelovich, *New Rules*.

proclaims, and brings about good for his people: "Happiness associates with blessing."[7] For this reason, we can endorse what the exegete Pierre Grelot says: "Thus the theme of happiness spans biblical revelation in its entirety."[8]

The Bible speaks of happiness in the present as well as in the future; the future it means is generally an earthly future, but occasionally post-terrestrial (towards the end of the Old Testament revelation). "Happiness is life, a life that was long identified with terrestrial life."[9] The Creator desires the happiness of his people: "The joys of human life are a part of God's promises to men."[10] Throughout its journey, Israel's aspirations were refined in a way that disclosed an inherent hierarchy. "God, the source of the wholesome joys of this life, offers the highest possible joys to His people: the joys which are found in fidelity to the covenant."[11] Therefore, at the top of its values Israel places obedience to the Law and union with God, in response to a divine promise and in faithfulness to the Covenant. These moral and religious dimensions of happiness prove to be very important, encompassed within a wisdom for which "Life is something precious"[12] and "Life is fragile"[13] are complementary affirmations.

Christianity and Happiness

The great novelty introduced by Christianity is the Incarnation: "And the Word became flesh and lived among us" (John 1:14). According to the New Testament, the corollary of the Incarnation is

7. Article on "Bonheur" in Monloubou and Buit, *Dictionnaire biblique universel*, 94 (see 93–94).

8. Grelot, "La révélation du bonheur," 5 (see 5–35).

9. Article on "Beatitude" in Léon-Dufour, *Dictionary of Biblical Theology*, 45 (see 45–47). See also "Blessing," 47–51, and "Peace," 411–14.

10. Article on "Joy" in Léon-Dufour, *Dictionary of Biblical Theology*, 275 (see 275–77).

11. Article on "Joy" in Léon-Dufour, *Dictionary of Biblical Theology*, 275.

12. Article on "Life" in Léon-Dufour, *Dictionary of Biblical Theology*, 313.

13. Article on "Life" in Léon-Dufour, *Dictionary of Biblical Theology*, 313.

the divine status of believers: "But to all who received him, who believed in his name, he [the Word] gave power to become children of God" (John 1:12); ". . . it is that very Spirit bearing witness with our spirit that we are children of God, and if children, then heirs, heirs of God and joint heirs with Christ" (Rom 8:16–17).

Compared to Judaism, this strongly accentuates the properly religious dimension of happiness. While it is true, as we saw, that this dimension appears in the Hebrew Bible, it occupies a much larger place in the New Testament: God offers an intimacy that goes all the way to sharing his own life. As Jacques Pohier emphasizes:

> [T]here is scarcely any religion, ideology or culture that has promised such happiness and such glory to humans. While numerous religions have promised humans at least some sharing in divine life, none has taken this as far as Christianity. As the New Testament emphatically demonstrates, this exceeds anything that human hearts could have conceived.[14]

Later we shall see what implications the author draws from this specific quality of the message of Jesus, when we look at the issue of rigour or scruples. Here let us note that one aspect of happiness is of enormous importance: the matter of participating in divine life. In fact, it is such a key aspect that henceforth we will employ the term "beatitude," which mirrors its Latin origins. Using this particular term will also help us to discuss the relationships between this "beatitude" and the other components of happiness.

As soon as Christianity began to spread in the Roman Empire, it encountered the eudemonism of antique wisdom. This noble quest for happiness took a variety of forms, the main ones being a Platonic spiritualism oriented towards contemplation of the invisible Good; Aristotelian virtue comprising knowledge of philosophical and scientific truth and the pursuit of justice in friendship; Stoical detachment with its concentration on inner peace; and the moderated, orderly Epicurean search for pleasure. But these tendencies demonstrate a common trait, namely an

14. Pohier, *Au nom du Père*, 196.

intellectual sort of wisdom; so they are too aristocratic to be embraced by the majority of people.

Nevertheless, the great Christian thinkers of antiquity and the Middle Ages wanted to define beatitude as introduced by Christ in relation to Greco-Latin happiness. They provided a hierarchy to establish this relationship. Beatitude—given fully in the future life but anticipated here below—is at the summit of the goods that God gives to humans. The other goods are inferior and subordinate to it, and they have their own hierarchy; based on Plato and Aristotle, it puts biological pleasures at the bottom, mental life in the middle, and spiritual activities on top. Reflecting their Christianity and their Jewish heritage and wishing to accept what is good from the wisdom of antiquity, Augustine and Aquinas proposed respect combined with detachment regarding earthly things. Highly conscious of the fragility of human existence in the waning phase of the Roman Empire, Augustine accentuated eternal beatitude and upheld hope as the fundamental attitude to take in a world marked by suffering, illness, and death. Thomas, by contrast, living in a period of economic prosperity and social and cultural creativity, has a less pessimistic outlook than his predecessor and recognizes the possibility of imperfect worldly happiness.

While they grapple with new questions posed by the presence of ancient wisdom, the theological syntheses of the patristic and medieval epochs fully respect the major points of the New Testament. They regard the great gift of filial adoption with awe, while earthly happiness is relativized but not repudiated. This is the classical position in Catholic theology, which subordinates earthly happiness to beatitude. We will return to this in the last section of the present chapter.

Moral Laxity

History has given us two other Christian positions on happiness: laxity and rigour. Hardly any theologians have defended the first, but the term (laxity) might characterize practices in some churches.[15] The second was proposed as the Christian ideal by theologians belonging to austere movements such as Montanism,[16] Jansenism,[17] and Puritanism.[18] The fact that laxity and rigour have attracted many followers leads us to suspect that they respond to tendencies that are deeply rooted in humans—so much so as to deform Christianity.

Laxity comes to the fore in historical periods that are considered as times of decadence. This applies equally well to the worldly Catholicism of the Italian Renaissance and to "à la carte" religion in the West at the start of this twenty-first century.[19] Nowadays, even among people who self-identify as Christians, we find attitudes that are closer to a Christian-hued psychologism than a real understanding of the gospel ideal. In large part, such dilutions of Christianity into a religion of pleasure and personal growth are reactions against Christian rigorism.

Rigorism

Rigorism manages to penetrate Christianity in all eras. But the fourteenth and fifteenth centuries were especially fertile times: the Hundred Years' War, the Black Death, suppression of heresies and sorcery, the debauchery and avarice of clergy at all levels, and the Great Schism in the Western Church led to violence, decadence, pessimism, and guilt.[20] When Luther appeared early in the sixteenth century, concrete conditions favoured a theological

15. See "Laxisme," in Vacant et al., *Dictionnaire de théologie catholique*, vol. 9, I, 37–39.

16. See "Montanisme," in Viller et al., *Dictionnaire de spiritualité*, vol. 10, 1674.

17. See "Jansénisme," in Viller et al., *Dictionnaire de spiritualité*, vol. 8, 139–44.

18. Especially in its insistence on strict and austere observance of the Sabbath. See "Sabbatarianism" in McDonald, *New Catholic Encyclopedia*, vol. 12, 777–78.

19. See Bibby, *Fragmented Gods*.

20. See Leclercq et al., *La spiritualité*, 573–93.

interpretation opposed to the traditional Catholic synthesis. The religious question of the moment was essentially about sin and individual salvation.[21] Whereas peace (*shalom*) in Judaism consists in being whole, complete, and integrally human[22] (that is, in good moral and physical health) thanks to God's help, the sixteenth-century Reformation disconnected salvation from happiness. Even well into the twentieth century, Protestantism promoted mistrust of happiness. As tables of contents (and the index, if provided) demonstrate, happiness is not mentioned by the major theologies of the Old Testament.[23] For its part, Catholicism fared no better when it allowed itself to be influenced by Jansenism. But since rejection of happiness proves to be humanly impracticable, one finds instances of backsliding—apparently unconscious, but blazingly obvious to observers with a minimum of psychological sophistication. In fact, rigorism almost always ends in pitiful internal division. It can also happen that persons burdened by frustration may compensate in various ways, such as an anxious search for recognition, a wish for power, or a wish to dominate; or, guilty for their feelings of happiness, they may insist upon sacrifices that bear no constructive relationship to their family and societal situation. The renunciation of happiness by numerous Christians is a bankruptcy that has done much to discredit Christianity among our contemporaries.

In the last chapter of a work already mentioned,[24] Jacques Pohier takes pains to provide a psychoanalytical and theological explanation of rigorism, which in the Latin Church has mainly targeted sexuality. He shows this in three steps.

In the first place, because pleasure occurs as a complete whole and concentrated in the moment, it readily serves as an image of happiness. Nevertheless, every intelligent person knows that

21. See Delumeau, *Le péché*.

22. See "Peace" in Léon-Dufour, *Dictionary of Biblical Theology*, 411–12 (see 411–14 for context).

23. See Eichrodt, Jacob, van Imschoot, von Rad, and Vriezen.

24. Pohier, *Au nom du Père*, chapter 5: "Recherche sur les fondements de la morale sexuelle chrétienne."

pleasure cannot pass for happiness, it is not the same as happiness. This is because pleasure is circumscribed, whereas happiness does not have precise limits of intensity and duration. The inevitable disappointment is not easy to bear—which leads to the temptation to turn against pleasure and even to condemn it:

> Everything seems in effect to come to this—as if the only way to demystify this hypostasis of pleasure is to reproach pleasure for being what it is and to deny its authentic value, on the pretext that pleasure is not what we expect it out to be . . . Ultimately we say that it is nothing because we are afraid to say that it is everything.[25]

Second, Pohier adds certain psychoanalytical observations to these thoughts on the ambiguity of pleasure and happiness. He begins by noting that the experience of masculinity and femininity is a search for completion and power, which uncovers the incompleteness and powerlessness in every individual. In the Oedipal relationship, which persists even when the complex has been fairly well resolved, the child (boy or girl) desires the phallus, which is to say, paternal power. Since the sexual object that consists of the parent of the other sex remains inaccessible because of taboo, the subject is in an ambivalent situation. The subject needs the power and protection of the father on the one hand, and on the other, wishing to take over the father's exclusive privilege, the subject feels resentful and afraid of him. Accordingly, sexuality proves to be the context par excellence where the thirst for life and the fear of death coexist in dramatic fashion.

Third, it happens that two beliefs in Christianity actually buttress a rejection of pleasure, especially sexual. These concern eschatology and the cross. The expectation of an incomparably better world and participation in the supreme sacrifice of Jesus can favour the renunciation of pleasure; and they can serve as pretexts for avoiding the painful ambiguities of bodily life. According to a certain understanding of the Paschal Mystery, in order to overturn the revolt of the first son (Adam), who tried to appropriate divine

---

25. Pohier, *Au nom du Père*, 184.

omnipotence, the second son (Christ) must submit as victim to the father's anger. In this soteriology of substitution, the sons recover, as if by magic, the immortality that they first wanted to steal from God.

It is not very difficult to work out analogies between this incorrect interpretation of Christian salvation and the dramatic script of the Oedipus complex.[26] Truly, this sort of search for salvation, connected to a negative image of God, constitutes an obsessive repetition of original sin. It is antithetical to the compassionate welcome of a free and loving gift from a Creator who is not jealous but simply wishes to share the best of himself.

A Hierarchy

Accordingly, when it is not contaminated by laxity or rigorism, Christianity proposes a hierarchy among pleasure, happiness, and beatitude. Prominent among pleasures are those of the senses, along with the extraordinary ways that human society embellishes them. The pleasures of shared meals and of sports, to mention two cases, are enhanced by a heightened meaning conveyed to the senses. Beyond these pleasures that flow from biological vitality, we find a wider sense of pleasure associated with satisfaction from the accomplishment of valuable activities. Such activities take place in numerous contexts: family, work, leisure, art, intellectual life, religion, etc.

Comparing pleasure to happiness, Antoine Vergote writes:

> It appears that happiness is a more encompassing state than pleasure, as the latter deals with a delimited satisfaction . . . By itself, the search for pleasure does not bring happiness; but the happy man is able to take pleasure in a diversity of activities and encounters. Indeed, the capacity for pleasure is the sign of a state of happiness, just as the frantic pursuit of pleasures indicates that a person is not happy.[27]

26. See Pohier, *Au nom du Père*, 219.

27. Vergote, "Plaisir, désir, bonheur," 37.

What, then, of this happiness that goes beyond pleasures while it integrates them? It is a state of the soul, enduring joy, permanent peace. Unlike the illusory happiness that stems from awkward relationships with others, true happiness is the fruit of a good ethical orientation. Happiness is there for every individual who lives according to important values and knows how to apply them wisely.

It is easy to fall into the pursuit of false happiness. All that is required is to treat a properly relative value as absolute: money, security, sexuality, autonomy, success, justice, etc. Happiness requires detachment from one's own self and one's values. Furthermore, our happiness cannot be authentic if our hearts and minds are closed to the unhappiness of so many of our sister and brother human beings. But how is it possible to keep our eyes open to evil and misfortune and continue the endless battle against suffering and injustice? And how to prevent the hard fight against evil from turning into a form of individual or group idolatry—feelings of superiority, lust for power, control that is blind to freedoms, favouritism, and so on?

The aim of these questions is to highlight the role that beatitude can play with respect to happiness. If beatitude is properly understood and well lived, it consists in a fullness felt either as great joy (when external circumstances are favourable) or as profound peace (when circumstances are unfavourable). This fullness coexists with total acceptance of dissatisfaction, because Christian hope approaches temporality (which is necessarily tinged with dissatisfaction) as an opportunity to grow in love. This dynamic of fullness-dissatisfaction promotes the detachment of believers from self and from idols, and their engagement with values and against evil.

Thus, just as pleasures are subordinate to happiness, the latter is equally subordinate to beatitude. Earthly happiness as a permanent state or disposition is not an absolute. Love alone is the absolute: it modulates happiness by its consent to open one's eyes to suffering, to feel inevitable sadness in the face of varied forms of human privation, and to act according to one's conscience.

3

Beyond Optimism and Pessimism

Is it possible to know intense joy while avoiding optimism and pessimism?—"intense joy" in the sense of happiness as conveyed in the beatitudes of Jesus; optimism like that of Jean-Jacques Rousseau, which colours contemporary humanistic psychology; and pessimism in response to violence and the ecological threat facing our world.

The gospel has redefined itself constantly throughout its long dialogue with cultures. In this third millennium, Western Christianity is compelled to clarify its identity principally in relation to culture that is preoccupied with the psychological. This compels us to show how a particular psychology of optimistic hue influences the way many adherents see their religion. Recalling the origin of this optimism in Rousseau and humanistically oriented psychologists will expose the difference between Rousseau's belief in the fundamental goodness of human beings, which can never be lost, and the greater depth and nuance of biblical revelation as developed through Thomism. According to this Jewish and Catholic tradition, Christianity ought not to be characterized as either optimistic or pessimistic but as a realism tinged with great overriding hope.

On Human Potential

Two tendencies are found in modern psychology. The first, quite pessimistic, starts with Freud. Then comes a decidedly optimistic tendency, which corresponds to the highly diverse current—neither Freudian nor behaviourist, and humanistic in orientation—that Abraham Maslow calls the third force.[1] Stretching from Jung to New Age, this is a largely North American trend. And what justifies our considering it to be an optimistic tendency is its very high regard for human potential, seen as vast and even unlimited.

Echoing what they have learned from North American psychology, contemporary apologists for faith—theologians and pastoral agents—affirm that Catholicism, unlike the Protestantism of Luther and Calvin, is fundamentally optimistic. They suggest (wrongly, I believe) that Augustine was a pessimist while Aquinas would be an optimist. Moreover, they explain, many Christians over two millennia have been pessimists. But true Catholicism— that of Aquinas and Vatican II—would be optimistic. On this point, moreover, they find it encouraging to note that the Thomist vision of human nature (like that of liberal Protestantism) is almost the same as that of humanistic psychology.

The intentions of this effort to separate Christian faith from pessimism are certainly to be praised. But the Jansenist slant of Catholicism that Quebeckers knew for sixty-plus years is regrettable. It was wrong to conflate the gospel with Jansenist pessimism. But what of the opposite, putting Christianity into the company of optimism of various stripes: would that not risk a similar confusion?

The Origins of Modern Optimism

Jean-Jacques Rousseau (1712–1778) appears to have initiated the modern optimist trend. He writes: "The fundamental principle of all morality . . . is that man is a naturally good being, loving justice

---

1. Maslow, *Religions*, 69–71.

and order; that there is no original perversity in the human heart, and that the first movements of nature are always right."[2]

The remainder of the text explains that external conditions lead humans to be depraved. The author pins his hopes on education as the way to restore the integrity of individuals. However, concern for oneself comes first. Hence his maxim "Do what is good for you with as little harm as possible to others."[3] The variant that one hears nowadays in church circles is "trust others and they'll do just fine." According to Rousseau and his modern disciples, one may count on the good reflexes of others on condition one knows how to deal with them. One gathers that appropriate attitudes and competent pedagogy make the belief in original sin obsolete, along with the redemption achieved by Jesus Christ.

Rousseau's optimism arises in reaction to the Calvinist interpretation that darkens human nature. In this same vein Maslow declares: "Human nature is not nearly as bad as it has been thought to be."[4] Further, "The basic needs (for life, for safety and security, for belongingness and affection, for respect and self-respect, and for self-actualization), the basic human emotions and the basic human capacities are on their face either neutral, pre-moral or positively 'good.'"[5]

Later we shall see that there is a difference between neutrality and moral goodness. At this point we note that Maslow's solution, like his diagnosis, is highly similar to that of Rousseau. He explains:

> How can we encourage free development [of personality]? What are the best educational conditions for it? Sexual? Economic? Political? What kind of world do we need for such people to grow in? What kind of world will such people create? Sick people are made by a sick culture; healthy people are made possible by a healthy culture.[6]

2. Rousseau, *Letter to Beaumont*, 28.

3. Rousseau, "Discourse," 25–109, at 55.

4. Maslow, *Toward a Psychology*, 5.

5. Maslow, *Toward a Psychology*, 5.

6. Maslow, *Toward a Psychology*, 7.

Of course we can act—we must act—in all the contexts that Maslow lists. The question remains, however, whether Christianity has something to add regarding human pathology.

Sheep and Goats

Contrary to Rousseau's thesis of the inalienable natural goodness of human beings, the Bible sets forth a claim that is rather shocking to our modern ears: as a matter of fact, some humans are good while others are bad (the sheep and the goats, Matt 25:31–46). Even the declaration in the first chapter of Genesis—"God saw everything that he had made, and indeed, it was very good" (Gen 1:31)—gives no grounds for thinking that the human person would always remain fundamentally good. What the first chapter of Genesis strongly affirms is that in the beginning, by the power of the divine Word, the first couple as created were resplendent in their goodness. The third chapter, however, tells of the loss of this original goodness; and the rest of the Book of Genesis emphasizes human perversity (for example, Cain, the people at the time of Noah and the flood, and the brothers of Joseph).

What underpins this difference between some individuals who are morally good and others who are morally misguided? The answer in Ezekiel is the presence or absence of a stable inclination towards the good (heart of flesh and heart of stone, Ezek 11:19; 36:26). And one finds *agapē* in those whom the New Testament calls "the saints"—so strong a disposition to love God and others that it can accept the sacrifices that accompany the exercise of this charity. Against this, Jesus points out the contrary disposition to his disciples when he says, ". . . the world hates you," ". . . they have no excuse for their sin," "They hated me without a cause" (John 15:18–25).

The Thomist theology of grace holds that those who respond "yes" to the Holy Spirit are good at heart; those who reply "no" have a wicked heart. The sin of malice exists: it can happen that an evil intention carries the day amidst the complexity of motives that influence a decision and may even excuse it up to a certain point

("They do not know what they are doing," Luke 23:34). It is the attraction of apparent goods that invites such absurd capitulation to evil (knowing that it will be harmful to others). As Aquinas noted, one does not aim directly at doing evil: "No one does evil except intending some good as it appears to him . . . The will is moved to something which is good in some respect." The example he gives is adultery, an evil with which a certain good is associated, that of sensual pleasure.[7]

Apparent goods are not sought in isolation. They connect with values that are poorly understood and attach poorly to goods. These values turn into anti-values because of the idolatrous context in which they are exalted to excess. As Augustine saw full well, the supreme value of the God of Love is replaced by secondary values such as success, self-image, reputation, position, and influence over others.

No Neutral Middle Ground

Depending on the fundamental choices they make, adults are either good or bad. There is no neutral position, even if the good-hearted person occasionally shows a lack of love and if the wicked-hearted person sometimes helps another human being[8] (whether for noble or selfish motives). The only aspect of human nature that always remains morally neutral is its fundamental constitution—what allows us to act, whether wisely or in a disordered manner. Because it is purely open to the real good and to apparent goods equally, human nature is neither good nor bad in itself. In other words, in its fundamental constitution, the human nature of every individual remains morally neutral; but the concrete individual becomes either good or bad according to the individual's choice for or against divine love.

One text of Aquinas seems to suggest a certain confidence in the human person: "But even after sin there still remains in the

---

7. Aquinas, *On Evil*, q. 1, a. 3.

8. Aquinas, *Summa Contra Gentiles*, book III, chapter 160.

human soul a potentiality of good, because the natural powers, whereby the soul is related to its proper good, are not taken away by sin."[9] This affirmation seems optimistic so long as we ignore that here the word "potency" has a weak, typically Aristotelian sense: merely capacity for acting, merely openness to receiving an excellence. It is not about power in the modern sense of being able to act thanks to one's own strengths alone. Moreover, the context speaks of a human potency which is "reducible to act by the active power of God." It is also said of the human soul that "God can confer . . . the grace that puts the recipient in the state of grace."[10] Finally, the titles of two adjoining chapters reaffirm these human limits: "That Man cannot be delivered from Sin except by Grace"[11] and "That a Man already in Mortal Sin cannot avoid more Mortal Sin without Grace."[12]

It is important, therefore, to distinguish between fundamental constitution and actual persons. On the one hand, the fundamental constitution is morally neutral; on the other hand, persons are either good at heart or wicked. This is why Aquinas would accept the claim that the human being as such is basically good, in an ontological sense, or in the order of creation—we will return to this in chapter 8—but not in the moral sense. If we took this in the moral sense, we would confuse the optimism of Pelagius, Rousseau, and many psychologists with the realism of Augustine and Aquinas. The latter is a realism that is pessimistic about the possibilities of the concrete individual; yet it becomes full of hope due to its confidence in the grace offered to all by Christ.

Moreover, one can never judge with complete certainty that a person is evil at heart. It may be true of some individuals: there are actual people—Hitler, Stalin, those behind the massacres in Bosnia, those who abuse children, adolescents, and young women in work, prostitution, and slavery; there are the fictional characters of literature and opera such as Medea, Lady Macbeth, Iago. Yet

9. Aquinas, *Summa Contra Gentiles*, book III, chapter 157.
10. Aquinas, *Summa Contra Gentiles*, book III, chapter 157.
11. Aquinas, *Summa Contra Gentiles*, book III, chapter 158.
12. Aquinas, *Summa Contra Gentiles*, book III, chapter 161.

love demands that we hope and pray for all people, however horrendous their crimes might be. Furthermore, humility demands that all believers to whom God has given a good heart (sanctifying grace) should pray for the gift of the Holy Spirit to maintain their orientation towards the good, in collaboration with their human liberty.

Christianity Is Hope

Neither "optimism" nor "pessimism" applies to Christianity. Optimism holds that human beings are always good in spite of their moral shortcomings, these being attributed either to error (Plato) or to deviance that arises from education and society (Rousseau, followed by numerous twentieth-century psychologists). Optimism proclaims that to the extent that we improve the circumstances leading to critical choices, we can count on the goodness of human will, which never loses its capacity to respond well.

When Christianity is merged with the optimistic vision of life found in humanistic psychology, we risk taking a normative stand that ignores the need for specifically religious salvation, which is offered by Jesus Christ. On the other hand, when we acknowledge Christianity's alternative diagnosis of evil, we can make comparisons with psychology that respect the difference of Christianity rather than making everything the same. The dialogue between Christianity and psychology of an optimistic bent must allow for the differences as well as the overlaps.

Thus, through its long tradition that includes Vatican II, Catholicism holds that, with the exception of Jesus and Mary, all human beings are marked by sin and its negative consequences. Unlike optimism, it does not try to reassure us by having us believe that no matter what, we will retain our essential goodness. This is the realistic side of Catholicism, which it shares with pessimism. But unlike pessimism, it offers hope based on a historical fact: the liberating power of the human-and-divine love manifested in

Jesus Christ.[13] And once it is grasped in its originality, this religious hope has the capacity to integrate and synthesize the partial liberations of therapy and education.

Accordingly, the joy that flows from the beatitudes is rendered all the more powerful by the fact that its realism fully acknowledges evil—all the way to moral evil that can annihilate us—and by the fact that its hope firmly permeates all situations, however grim they may be, in order to live them differently.

13. See Roy, "Death of Jesus," 517–28.

4

Three Forms of Hope

EVERYDAY HOPE, RELIGIOUS HOPE, and Christian hope: these are the three forms of hope, and although inseparable, they are distinct. I will present them sequentially and show how the first leads to the second, and the second to the third. And since the first—everyday hope—is experienced to different degrees by all, it is well to begin there and to show that it cannot be fully realized until it becomes religious hope; just as the latter can only reach fullness when it becomes Christian hope.

Why take this approach to the subject? Because we live in a world where many people only know everyday hope, or religious hope. The best way to bring about better understanding of Christian hope is to compare it to the everyday and religious forms. In this way we will be better able to carry out the role of witnessing to which Saint Peter invites us when he writes: "Always be ready to make your defence to anyone who demands from you an account of the hope that is in you" (1 Pet 3:15).

Everyday Hope

In the first instance, hope is an everyday reality that is deeply rooted in humans, whatever their vision of the world and of life may be, and whether they are believers or not. Françoise Dolto states:

> At the moment of birth, every human being is filled with hope . . . Each time that hope arises in us—hope directed towards someone or towards a goal—our courage grows, our life finds direction, our endurance in the face of adversity becomes stronger . . . Hopelessness, loss of love, confidence shattered—these are the major difficulties that confront humans.[1]

How is hope manifested? True, hope has its ups and downs. Sometimes obstacles or setbacks can cause discouragement to hijack us and leave us mired in despondency. Nothing works anymore and we find ourselves without hope. Nevertheless, we sense that hopelessness and (even more so) despair are contrary to nature because they kill the life in us. This is why, after a difficult period, we generally take hold of ourselves and try to turn things round. We return to believing in ourselves, in our possibilities, our destiny; we tell ourselves that interesting moments may yet be found in daily life and our taste for life is restored. Often it is a friend who encourages us with some well-chosen words and especially by being there for us and offering us an understanding ear. Hope thus appears in new beginnings: after a period of dejection and sadness, we discover a sort of new energy, a shot in the arm. It reaches the point where everything seems relatively easy; we embark on new projects and we face the future with some measure of confidence.

Hope is necessary. We are made to hope; it is a condition for our living. We need to be more aware of this fundamental desire, of this dynamic within ourselves, and delve deeper into its meaning.

How is it that most people try constantly to improve their lot and that of those who are close to them? Why is it difficult to resign themselves to limitations in personality and their life? Does this mean that the aspirations of human beings are infinite? Balzac,

1. Dolto, *La foi*, 102.

observer extraordinaire of the human heart, wrote as follows about Colonel Chabert, one of his characters:

> Though he was eager in pursuit of his military distinction, of his fortune, of himself, perhaps it was in obedience to the inexplicable feeling, the latent germ in every man's heart, to which we owe the experiments of alchemists, the passion for glory, the discoveries of astronomy and of physics, everything which prompts man to expand his being by multiplying himself through deeds or ideas.[2]

This "inexplicable feeling" that impels a person to undertake projects and develop himself is manifest at the starting point of every human activity. Without this inexplicable feeling, there would be no action, science, art, religion—in brief, no human life.[3] Yet this feeling is merely a "latent germ in every man's heart." In effect, we can stifle the hope within just as we can make it grow.

Religious Hope

Without the "inexplicable feeling" of which Balzac speaks, without the natural hope that the Creator placed at the core of human beings, religion itself would not exist. Religion must properly be seen as an outgrowth of everyday hope, and we will approach religious hope in this perspective.

Hope is always unfulfilled—that is what we see all the time. Where indeed should we turn for contentment? Health, success, thought, beauty, justice? Even when what we achieve has great value, don't we remain conscious that our achievements are very limited? Why are our noblest desires never satisfied? If we never reach the goal of our efforts perfectly and if our existence ends at death, then, in the words of Sartre, would not man be "a useless passion"?[4]

---

2. Balzac, *Colonel Chabert*.

3. See Welte, *Qu'est-ce que croire?*, 28–29.

4. Sartre, *Being and Nothingness*, 754.

Augustine provides the key to this enigma in the following extraordinary phrase: "You have made us and drawn us to yourself, and our heart is unquiet until it rests in you."[5] It is vital to observe that what we are *immediately* conscious of is not that "you have made us and drawn us to yourself" but rather that "our heart is unquiet." Our hearts are constantly in a state of desire, expectation, and search: this is a fundamental phenomenon that all of us experience, believers and non-believers. It is a feature of everyday life with its responsibilities and exertions and worries. But to understand in a truly personal way how the starting point ("you have made us and drawn us to yourself") and the end point ("until it rests in you") connect with everyday life ("our heart is unquiet"), we need to probe and reflect.

The bridge between everyday life and the religious dimension of existence is provided by two very simple yet very profound questions about human hope: (1) From where does this hope come that propels my striving, that urges me every day to continue the battle of life? (2) And where am I being led by this hope that compels me perpetually to look for happiness? If I reply that my existence began and will end as matters of chance, don't I risk reducing my existence to some absurd vibration? But if I reply instead—audaciously, perhaps—that my hope has a Source and a Final End, I accord global meaning to it and a religious dimension. Then I can understand why I *am* hope, and I can proclaim with Augustine (varying his sentence slightly): if our heart is always restless, it is because you have made us for yourself, Lord, and our heart wishes to find rest in you.

Religious hope is therefore nothing but the extension of everyday hope. Religious hope is everyday hope that surpasses itself and opens up to its Source, to the one who made it and who alone can provide the foundation that gives it its true scope. Nothing is more daring than this everyday hope that becomes religious—that enters into relationship with its creator, in other words. Hope thus attains a sort of plenitude. It firmly believes that the Mystery which I nebulously desire is more than an idea, it truly exists, it is

5. Augustine, *Confessions*, book I, 1.

greater than me, and it is the origin of all goodness. It knows that divine love is flawless, that this love could not possibly fail. Like the Psalmist, it says "my rock" of the one on whom it can rely in complete confidence, in utter calm, throughout its journey on earth.

This, then, is religious hope. Not only does it understand the meaning of Augustine's phrase "you [Lord] have made us for yourself"; it also experiences the meaning of the ending of the sentence "until it rests in you."[6] This allows us to begin to savour the inner calm, the letting go, the peace that comes from trust in God. "Therefore I tell you," says Jesus, "do not worry about your life, what you will eat or what you will drink, or about your body, what you will wear. Is not life more than food, and the body more than clothing?" (Matt 6:25). Life is more than interest in earthly values; life is friendship with God. It is knowing that everything comes from him and everything goes to him; it is finding our joy in cultivating our sense of gift from God—of this creative act by which God gives us everything we are at every moment. It is recognizing our entire dependence on the one for whom we are made.

This religious hope, which completes everyday hope by giving it a solid and flawless foundation, is not limited to those who *proclaim* that they believe. Jesus emphasizes the difference between saying and doing: "Not everyone who says to me, 'Lord, Lord', will enter the kingdom of heaven, but only one who does the will of my Father in heaven" (Matt 7:21). And he illustrates this warning with his parable of the wise man who builds his house on rock. Many pseudo-believers build their lives on something other than union with God, because they place their hope elsewhere, on lesser values. By contrast, in practice, people who say they do not believe may well base their lives on love and thus cultivate hope that is religious in character.

Christian Hope

We just saw that religious hope—the hope of an individual who believes in God—goes farther than everyday hope, to which it

6. Augustine, *Confessions*, book I, 1.

provides support and the foundation. Let us turn now to the fact that Christian hope—the hope of an individual who believes in Jesus Christ—goes farther than religious hope, to which it equally provides support and the foundation. In these times when many people believe in God without believing in Jesus, that is, without acknowledging that Jesus is the Son of God and the Saviour, it is vital to define how our hope in Jesus Christ completes our hope in God.

Purely religious hope, which ignores the revelation of the Son of God, remains fragile in the face of evil. Of course, it teaches me that I come from the great Mystery and it allows me to trust that I am moving effectively towards it. Along the way, however, I struggle in a world marked by much suffering and I see that humans like me are affected by absurd tribulations: famine, war, disaster, illness, infirmity, reversals of fortune, psychological setback, social and political corruption, etc. The question cannot be avoided: Why does the good and almighty God do nothing to eliminate these misfortunes which undermine human persons so much? This is the question of the Psalmist, repeated a thousand times in Israel: "Why, O Lord, do you stand far off? Why do you hide yourself in times of trouble?" (Ps 10:1). This is truly the question that often shakes faith in the goodness, the power, or the personal character of God and which, as a consequence, puts religious hope to the test.

In addition to evil that is suffered, there is also the evil for which we are responsible, or with which we are complicit at the very least. This is called sin. And sin is not only this or that voluntary act; it also pertains to every instance of collusion in unjust conditions and all indifference towards those who suffer. We detect such collusion and indifference within ourselves, but we do not like to face up to them because they tarnish the image that we want to have of ourselves. It is not easy for us to acknowledge our solidarity with sin in the world. Of course, confronted by social injustice, we are sometimes ready to admit with Saint John that "the whole world lies under the power of the evil one" (1 John 5:19); nonetheless, we quite readily think that it is mostly the fault of others, and we ignore John's other phrase: "If we say that we have no sin, we deceive ourselves, and the truth is not in us" (1 John 1:8).

In sum, in the face of evil, we often find ourselves passive, resigned, and complicit. And we stay like this due to certain impediments, to our limits and weaknesses, and to our lack of confidence in ourselves and others. Therefore we need someone to come and rouse us, to restore light and courage and confidence to us. We need a prophet to speak to us in the name of God and tell us how God stands in relation to evil—and show us the path to follow.

In a single profound sentence, John's Gospel sums up what God does for a world that is lost and entangled in its sins: "God so loved the world that he gave his only Son, so that everyone who believes in him may not perish but may have eternal life" (John 3:16). Jesus came to announce the good news that an incomparable Kingdom was at hand: "The time is fulfilled, and the kingdom of God has come near; repent, and believe in the good news" (Mark 1:15). "The time is fulfilled": that is, the reign of God begins here below. The reign of love has been established once and for all by the death and resurrection of Jesus. Thanks to this salvation event, we can believe that our difficulties in this life have meaning, and they can be overcome and make us grow in love. Whatever the results anticipated or achieved, all our efforts, united with those of Christ, contribute from this moment forward to building the Kingdom that is so deeply desired.

This Christian hope, based on the teaching of Jesus, surpasses religious hope. The latter allows us to think that what follows death is not the void, because it is certain that a perfect state exists, to which we cannot help directing our hope. In addition to confirming this religious expectation and giving it greater precision, Christian hope assures us of a presence both human and divine; and not only beyond our death, but already in this life. If Jesus truly lived as a man, if he suffered for love, if he experienced the limits of human anguish, if he died, and if he triumphed over evil when the Father resurrected him, I can believe that I am never alone, whatever stage or condition of life I am in. Jesus Christ is always with me: Jesus, the human being who never withdraws his love from me; Christ, this divine Son whose Spirit of love is capable of giving me the strength to endure every sort of trial.

Whereas religious hope tends sometimes to look only towards the beyond—and it can happen, unfortunately, that some Christians neglect earthly values and responsibilities—Christian hope operates in the present. It knows that the Holy Spirit is active within the present world and that everything favourable to human progress helps to build the Kingdom of God. This Kingdom is at play in what Roger Schutz, the prior of Taizé, was inspired by the Epistle to the Hebrews to call "God's today."[7] A new creation emerges bit by bit through humanity's suffering. Christian hope dares to affirm that we are partners in constructing a most beautiful edifice—and though we are not aware of the full plan, we do know that God is its architect.

This Christian vision of our earthly existence has implications with regard to evil. We are not obliged to wage trench warfare against evil, while sensing that we never make any headway and that at bottom, things never get any better. No doubt it is salutary that each generation perceives that it is no better than its predecessor, because this is a matter of truth and humility. But if, from one generation to the next, human effort merely erects scaffolding which is destined to disappear from the worksite, it must be remembered that the Holy Spirit utilizes it to build the City of God. Through our daily routines, our works, our triumphs and failures, our existence is imbued with meaning in that we are contributing to the plan of Jesus, and that we ourselves and those we love will be associated eternally with the joy of the completed work.

In brief, then, God wishes us to live deeply the three forms of hope: everyday hope, which energizes our living in the present; religious hope, which puts us in relationship with our Source and our Final End; and Christian hope, which is based on the witnessing and presence of Jesus Christ, our Saviour.[8]

---

7. Schutz, *Vivre*. The relevant passage is Heb 3:7—4:11.

8. See also Roy, *Coherent Christianity*, 49–66.

5

Consecration of Desire

THERE IS A YEARNING deep within human beings which usually goes unobserved, not only by others but also by the one who desires. It is the longing to love deeply, totally, without division. The Creator put this sentiment in us before clarifying it with the command "You shall love the Lord your God with all your heart, and with all your soul, and with all your strength, and with all your mind; and your neighbour as yourself" (Luke 10:27). The deepest longing of the human heart is to give oneself. Pope John Paul II proclaimed it in Montreal's Olympic Stadium in 1984 when he told thousands of young people: "Life is worth living, and worth giving!"

Christianity demands this gift of self, this consecration to God, whatever one's situation in life might be. For example, Saint Paul leaves individuals free to discern what practical conditions favour their particular union with God: "I say this for your own benefit, not to put any restraint upon you, but to promote good order and unhindered devotion to the Lord" (1 Cor 7:35).

The Heart Which Does Not Give Itself

Among those who currently believe in God and also in Jesus, a good number do not realize that they may obstruct the call to give fully of themselves. Influenced by the ideal of self-actualization, many focus on what they find pleasing, on individual success, on personal growth. Risk is certainly a feature of these options. One might founder on these shoals; but it would be self-deceiving to try and avoid the risk by neglecting human growth. To the contrary! To be able to give of itself, desire must take possession of itself; it must clarify its options and become independent from the expectations of others. In order to have a self of my own to give, I must strengthen that self.

The problem for those who aspire to be Christians is to decide what comes first. In the Christian context, in effect, the challenge is to subordinate individual growth to the fundamental purposes of life. Self-realization should take place in a broader context than the quest for one's own well-being. When the New Testament speaks of the Kingdom of God, the Body of Christ, the heavenly Jerusalem, or the Vine with the Father as winegrower, it draws attention to a vast interpersonal collectivity that radically relativizes the self.[1]

The heart that does not give itself becomes closed, either in a superficial optimism or in a pessimism which keeps it from getting to the bottom of things. On the one hand, in her choices, the optimist adopts the attitude of the aesthete, who seeks first and foremost to be swept up in interesting activities and pleasurable relationships. She ignores the good that would be fitting in a given situation but would cost too much because it demands that she dare to face conflict or to pay sustained attention to the sometimes complicated needs of other individuals and groups. The wish to live well will lead a person to just "play along," instead of making sacrifices that might have positive results in a given situation.

On the other hand, the pessimist is content to carry out his duties mechanically, without putting all the quality into them that he could. What distinguishes him from the optimist is that he does not expect to obtain personal benefit from his work or his relationships. These two categories of people are nevertheless alike in

---

1. See Roy, *Self-Actualization*.

that they keep themselves sheltered from evil and remain distant, physically and psychologically, from those who suffer.

An Initial Reconciliation

The total engagement of desire requires a preliminary condition: full reconciliation with what we are, with our gifts and limitations. It is necessary to accept our personal history without reservation, to place it in relationship to the others who have influenced us and who have been influenced by us. In their wisdom and their holy scriptures, all the great religions, including Christianity, evince this fundamental intuition: the acceptance of destiny. For Christians, far from being impersonal, this destiny can be viewed as a highly paternal providence, one which respects human freedom and yet is capable of drawing good from any situation.

Some people want to dedicate themselves completely to God, without recognizing that they have not truly accepted their strengths and their weaknesses. In this way, their consecration can be a way of feeling successful from a religious standpoint, of admiring themselves, of remaining imprisoned in their ego, no matter how generous that ego may be. People in this condition then live the *ideal* of consecration instead of the *actuality* of consecration. They are interiorly divided, because they cannot but hanker after what they have discarded. For example, the fact of being attracted, indeed fascinated by what they have not yet experienced, signals that they have not sufficiently interiorized the self-esteem which renders sacrifice possible without pangs of regret.

When a person is conscious of this problem, one of the typical errors is to think that she ought to try out everything, multiply experiences, attempt to have her fill. What this amounts to, however, is the pursuit of quantity. The solution lies instead on the side of quality: reflecting on what she has become, looking back over her life, especially the times when she was genuinely loved, and reflecting on her life's deep value. At the end of such a spiritual quest, she may come to a stage where she can say in all honesty and no artificiality: "Throughout my successes and my joys, I see

that there has always been something missing. This lack is permanent. I accept this basic incompleteness in relation to fullness. I am
happy to be sure of what is essential and unconcerned about what
is variable."

It is not easy to accept one's particular path wholeheartedly,
to accept the consequences of the past upon the present and to pic-
ture the future with hope. This requires that we forgive others for
many things, forgive ourselves, and even forgive God.[2] But when
we fully embrace what we have become, with our strengths and
deficiencies, we find great joy in offering others a self that is really
worthwhile and unique. We strongly believe that, as a member of
the Body of Christ, we have received the grace of being a gift to
our brothers and sisters in our personhood, our presence, and our
actions.

Acceptance of the Negative

When we understand self-consecration properly, we see that it is
neither an impoverishment of human experience nor a flight from
reality. This is evident when we consider carefully what Jesus says
about his disciples and himself during a long prayer to his Father:
"Sanctify them in the truth; your word is truth. As you have sent
me into the world, so I have sent them into the world. And for
their sakes I sanctify (*consacre*) myself, so that they also may be
sanctified (*consacrés*) in truth" (John 17:17–19). Consecration requires that, in the light of revelation, we make truth flourish in the
midst of the world. So to consecrate oneself is to plunge into the
most challenging aspect of the human adventure.

What turns out to be difficult is to enter into the whole of
reality, that is to say, into both the negative and the positive. The
negative exists both within and outside us. By reconciling ourselves
with what the exterior world has made of us, we accept a major
portion of our reality. But this phase must extend into confrontation with the negative within ourselves. Thus there is a death and
a resurrection of desire. The desire that dies is the misguided one,

2. See Roy, *Coherent Christianity*, 58–66.

which flees from evil. It dies when we have had enough of always saying yes only to the positive and no to the negative. By saying no to the negative, one continues to fear it, to run away from it, and thereby to create all sorts of problems for oneself.

What helps to accept the negative coming from others is the discovery that this negative exists in ourselves, too, at least as a possibility. The saints know that they are sinners, not because most of them have committed execrable deeds, but because they have entertained, even for a short while, attitudes that might have induced them to perform harmful actions. Saints are perfectly aware of the fact that it is easy to fall into attitudes that can cause death, both for others and for themselves, the moment they succumb to such attitudes. Therefore, to say yes to God, one must experience the power of "no"; one must probe one's strength to say no. The logic of the no, as it were, leads to yes, to restoration, to conversion.

To say yes to the negative, knowing that God's providence employs it for our good and for the good of others, clearly does not abolish the duty of resisting evil, injustice, immorality. However, a far-reaching transformation flows from saying yes to the negative: it completely changes the way we fight evil. Paradoxically, the folly of the cross produces great wisdom in how we interpret the negative. From the cross we learn how to say yes to the interconnected totality of our lives, accepting not only the good that occurs but also the evil that touches us; we can forgo the restless quest for nothing but the positive and accept the pros and cons in our state of life, our work, our relationships.

Attachment-Detachment

To become whole, desire must grow and undergo purification. This process calls for two complementary movements: attachment to and detachment from desire.

By responding to events and through prayer, desire grows and becomes attached. We have already shown how a welcoming attitude towards whatever transpires, the negative no less than the positive, disposes us to total openness to all that life expects of us. When we resolve not to avoid the demands of reality, prayer promotes an intensification of desire, in attachment to God. If we allow ourselves to be seduced by the Mystery, we grow as beings-of-desire and become capable of simply desiring. We no longer desire this or that thing but the Holy Spirit itself. We desire the Spirit for ourselves, for others, for the Church: "how much more will the heavenly Father give the Holy Spirit to those who ask him!" (Luke 11:13).

Detachment leads to the purification of desire. Through faith, persons of desire discover that what is important is not acquiring this or that; rather, it is to be members of the Body of Christ and to focus on their mission. To make their proper and unique contributions, in accordance with God's will, they are ready to give up many possibilities. They know that Jesus invites them to be detached—but not just *partially*, because the point is not simply to imitate non-believers who, having a modicum of wisdom, practise a certain degree of detachment. Acting in synergy with the Holy Spirit, their Christian detachment aspires to be *total* with respect to their plans, their roles, their accomplishments, and their failures.

Purification of Desire

The detachment proper to desire is based on attachment to Christ and the life that he gained for us: "I came that they may have life, and have it abundantly" (John 10:10). There are two components to this attachment-detachment. First, like a major breakthrough, attachment-detachment embeds permanently in us. Next, with the return of old reflexes (particular cravings for and refusals of the negative), we engage in a long struggle, but we are confident and feel a certain calm. The first part is passive; it is produced by operative grace, it is pure gift of the Holy Spirit. The second part is active, and we speak of cooperative grace because what transpires is a collaboration between God and ourselves as we marshal the appropriate means to nourish the fundamental attitude of attachment-detachment.

This attitude is therefore based on a dual process of purification. First there is the passive purification through the action of the Holy Spirit, who alone plumbs our affectivity so as to heal and strengthen it: "Blessed are the pure in heart, for they shall see God" (Matt 5:8). Then there is an active purification: we learn how not to be completely immersed in the life of the senses; and we gain greater facility in handling the perceptions, enticements and repulsions, projections, fears, etc., which make up our daily lives: "Your eye is the lamp of your body. If your eye is healthy, your whole body is full of light" (Luke 11:36). Thus purity of heart requires a safeguarded heart,[3] a certain circumspection, a more precise assessment of our strengths and weaknesses. This undertaking will not be something defensive on condition that our motives coalesce in one central intention, that of allowing God to shape our will to his own. We agree to prune a rose bush whose branches extend in all directions, so that it will look good in a garden bigger than itself.

The consecration of human desire is the fruit of a basic choice: the choice to go to the very limits of desire's attraction to the Mystery. It entails accepting that we are seeking the Absolute and then drawing the necessary conclusions. Our willing is intensified and is unified by clinging to God, his presence, his will, and the mission he entrusts to us within his plan for universal salvation. In its resolve to conform to the will of God, desire contains something passionate, tenacious, almost ferocious: the determination to employ all available means to consecrate itself to God and to encourage the consecration of others to God. Yet this labour of faithfulness remains secondary compared to trust in Christ, which is based on the fact that he calls us to consecration and gives us his Spirit to accomplish it. The most secret aspiration of the human heart then becomes immensely powerful, in the certainty that the folly of the cross is the only answer suited to the enigma of desire, of evil, and of love.

---

3. See Viller et al., *Dictionnaire de spiritualité*, vol. 4, "Garde du cœur," 100–17, and "Garde des sens," 117–22.

6

A Path towards Mystery

Human desire is open to Mystery by its very nature; open to a Reality which prompts its seeking, draws it forward, and always escapes it. Grappling with its enigmatic character, desire turns first to awe and questioning. Further, desire may subsequently acquire a special quality of consciousness. The first of these two stages is reflective; the second, experiential.

Our Amazing Desire

Desire wonders first at its capacity for knowing. We humans realize that our wish to connect with what surrounds us, to understand what is presented to us, to adhere to what is true, is not completely satisfied by action or art or the natural or human sciences. Our intelligence asks questions about itself: about the origin and possible goal of its very dynamism. The painter Paul Gauguin inscribed three fundamental questions on one of his huge Polynesian canvases: "Where do we come from? What are we? Where are we going?"

Desire also wonders at its capacity for entering into union. We sense that our need for personal interchange cannot be met entirely on a horizontal plane. True, by their presence and actions, others contribute enormously to awakening us to our own worth and desirability. But every individual remains free in the acceptance and exercise of this internal desire—desire which he does not spawn himself and which others arouse only from the outside. Far from being able to trigger his affections, he experiences them as a spring that wants to flow. Hence the question, not always formulated but ready for anyone with the least bit of lucidity in regard to his own affectivity: where does the source of my spring lie, and in what direction do its waters flow?

Our wonder bears, then, as much on the cognitive as on the affective side of desire.

Invitation to Mystery

In spite of normal reserve before the Infinite—which intimidates and attracts us at the same time—curiosity about the enigma of desire can draw us towards an experience of Mystery. In regard to God, why be satisfied with knowledge and feelings? Aren't these limited and inadequate? Might we be able to enter into intimacy with Mystery and encounter it as the Other? A strange fascination impels brave explorers to go beyond the habitual forms of consciousness.

Still, the route is full of ambushes, and very few dare to go forward alone in this adventure. If they take the attraction of the Mystery seriously, it is usually because they are encouraged by the witness of others who have preceded them along the paths to life according to the Spirit. There are masters who invite us to go beyond an essentially verbal, image-laden, or reflective way of searching for God. The fulfilment and balance these masters seem to enjoy incite many to become their followers. And for those who have no opportunity to find such a guide, a rich spiritual literature is waiting on the shelves of bookshops and libraries.

The Belgian Carmelite Wilfrid Stinissen emphasizes the longing of a number of our contemporaries for objectless meditation. He softens a little—rightly, in my opinion—the traditional point of view according to which one becomes ready for a more passive contemplation only after having actively engaged in object-oriented meditation. He reminds us that "there are many today who are too tired and distracted to practise object-oriented meditation." He explains: "They do not feel drawn that way, and if they try it, they fail. Their wanting to learn meditation is precisely in order to achieve calmness."[1] Basing himself on the fact that prayer is essentially participation in the life of the Trinity, that it is a gift of the Holy Spirit who intercedes for us (Rom 8:26) rather than "something we actively manage to do," he considers it possible even for beginners "to devote themselves from the first to objectless meditation."[2]

Stinissen clarifies what he means by objectless meditation by distinguishing "object-less" from "content-less." "Object-less" means the absence of something over against us, when we leave the subject-object distinction. Yet Christian prayer is not "contentless," for one knows oneself to be in "a concrete relationship of love with God." Stinissen takes up the expression "loving attention," employed by John of the Cross following Ruusbroec and Tauler, in reference to the unification of desire.[3] One thus escapes the boundaries of objects in order to enter into another form of consciousness: "In the depths of our being we are conscious, in a global and diffuse way, that we are desire for God—or we are adoration—or that we allow ourselves to be filled by God's love."[4]

It is also striking that Christian mystical authors invoke the Bible as a place where they find an invitation to constant prayer. This is the case, for example, of the author of *The Pilgrim's Tale*, who earnestly wonders about the way to put into practice Saint Paul's exhortations "Pray without ceasing," "Pray in the Spirit at all times in every prayer and supplication," "[I]n every place the men should pray, lifting up holy hands" (1 Thess 5:17; Eph 6:18; 1 Tim 2:8).[5]

---

1. Stinissen, *Méditation*, 168–69. For an English-language presentation of this author's themes, see Stinissen, *Gift*.

2. Stinissen, *Méditation*, 169.

3. Stinissen, *Méditation*, 156–57.

4. Stinissen, *Méditation*, 158–59.

5. Pentkovsky, *Pilgrim's Tale*, 49.

Forms of Consciousness

By consciousness I do not mean primarily moral consciousness, namely conscience, but rather, more generally, the fact of our being present to the world and to our own selves. Human consciousness consists of a twofold attending: to the world and to itself. These two aspects of attention are concomitant; our interest in reality is accompanied by immediate presence to ourselves as active subjects who are thus interested.

The consciousness that governs daily life is extroverted: we observe, understand, imagine, react to emotions, remember, ask questions, analyze, discuss, pass judgment, make decisions. This consciousness, however, takes a more disinterested turn when it becomes scientific or artistic. For example, the scientific spirit removes itself from immediate needs and compels us to get to know data independently of their usefulness. Or again: the painter's eye and the musician's ear catch, in shapes or sounds, possibilities which are unusual and free.

Whether it be pragmatic, scientific, or artistic, ordinary consciousness operates on a horizontal plane. There is, however, another form of consciousness, a vertical kind, which underpins the first. Let us call it religious consciousness or, more precisely, mystical consciousness. Although it can be accompanied by extraordinary phenomena, in itself mystical consciousness turns out to be something very simple.[6]

Some Features of Mystical Consciousness

Three features of mystical consciousness are worth noting. To begin with, it is characterized by *centredness*. It is centred, focused, simple. It coincides with dissatisfaction about thoughts and feelings in prayer. One becomes indifferent to the complexity of images, feelings, memories, logical connections. The conviction that God is found beyond every external relation reduces one's cognitive activity to a minimum; sometimes it disappears altogether.

6. See Roy, *Mystical Consciousness*.

The Holy Spirit invades the person and makes her enter into the mystery of the Trinity. Because God dwells in the deep centre of the human self, there is awareness of a loving union, even an identity with the Mystery, given to us in our assimilation into the body of Christ.

Secondly, mystical consciousness involves *detachment* in regard to myself, meaning that my "I" is present but forgets itself: "It is no longer I who live, but it is Christ who lives in me" (Gal 2:20a). This detachment is not an absence of interests or preferences, but a relativization of attachments arising from intensification of a desire that is inclined towards a truly religious mode of consciousness, given in germ at baptism and called to develop in a mystical way. Centring on God as Mystery entails decentring in regard to ourselves, to persons we would use as psychological crutches, and to every value which could function as an idol. This suggests that what is of primary importance is not the individual trying to self-construct by his own strength; rather, it is the whole of humanity being called to penetrate into the great Mystery.

Finally, mystical consciousness is accompanied by *gratitude*. It arises with recognition of the Triune God: the Creator who has made us beings-of-desire, desiring and desirable; the Redeemer who gives us his Son to heal our wounded desire, which has become ambivalent and distracted; and the Sanctifier who sends us the Spirit to establish religious consciousness within us, which is destined to blossom into mystical consciousness. From gratitude flows an increase of love as well as joy and peace, which alternate within us according to circumstances. The thanksgiving which is the Eucharist expresses this basic sentiment.

Rereading Cassian

The three characteristics of mystical consciousness recounted above can already be found in Cassian, a fifth-century spiritual master, who emphasizes the unification of the person around a goal, the purification which follows, and the grace that alone makes this process possible. I would encourage all to read (or reread) the first interview in this author's *Conferences*, where the message of Abbot Moses provides an entry point into the Mystery.[7]

Abbot Moses proposes a distinction in Christian life between end and goal (chap. II–V). The end (*telos* in Greek, *finis* in Latin) is the terminus, the arrival point, of the human pilgrimage on earth: the Kingdom of God, eternal life. The goal (*skopos* in Greek, *destinatio* in Latin) is the path, the manner of travelling, the incessant activity on which one concentrates. In the domain of agriculture, for example (chap. II–IV), the farmer who wants an abundant harvest (the end) will come back every day to the demanding work of preparing the soil (the goal).

The word "target" would be a better translation of the Greek *skopos* and the Latin *destinatio* than "goal." Another comparison given by Abbot Moses, that of the archer (chap. V), shows the difference between a prize to be won (the end) and that at which the archer aims with the bow (the goal, the target). The target is, then, the type of action one firmly wants and fixes upon, "the soul's goal and the mind's constant intention," the "one mark" towards which all efforts converge (chap. IV). The language of phenomenology provides an equivalent, namely *intending*; psychology speaks of *centring*, optics of *focal point*, and film of *focusing*.

If I multiply images, it is in order to try to sketch that state of mind which leads to mystical consciousness. Cassian calls it *purity of heart* (chap. V), the *charity* which flourishes in detachment (chaps. VI and XI). His Abbot Moses says: "This should be constantly pursued as the fixed goal of our heart, so that our mind may always be attached to divine things and to God" (chap. VIII). This is the ideal: "To cling to God unceasingly and to remain inseparably united to him by contemplation." And the condition is clear: "We ought to know where we should fix our mind's attention and to what goal we should always recall our soul's gaze" (chap. XIII).

In sum, although Cassian does not speak here in terms of consciousness, he presents the way in which desire is unified by making for itself a *destinatio*, that is, a firm resolution to be centred on a target. And the other *Conferences* make us understand that

7. Cassian, *Conferences*; references are given in my text.

this is attained only by totally relativizing the images and feelings proper to ordinary consciousness.

Mystical Consciousness and the Everyday

Our ordinary or everyday consciousness is horizontal; it consists in presence to the world and presence to self. Mystical consciousness is vertical; it finds the Mystery in the depths of the self. Because one type is horizontal and the other vertical, these two forms of consciousness, far from being in competition, coexist and even interpenetrate. Mystical consciousness enters ordinary consciousness, not usually to interfere with it but to enrich it. It brings a special quality to ordinary consciousness: calm, detachment, patience, a renewed capacity for listening to and loving the other, an increased dynamism in the pursuit of objectives aligned with the will of God.

When it moves from wondering about Mystery to the experience of Mystery, human desire reaches the level of consciousness called mystical consciousness. Dissatisfied now with ordinary consciousness, desire is intensified, and by grace it receives a consciousness that is properly divine. Not without fear, it is disposed to renounce a great deal in order to allow this divine consciousness grow within in. The gospel warns us that we must leave everything behind. In compensation, when all has been relativized, it will be given back a hundredfold, according to Jesus' promise, so that all can be fully enjoyed. When mystical consciousness permeates ordinary consciousness, it bestows an unexpected sweetness.

7

Dissatisfaction

FOR MANY PEOPLE, TOTAL satisfaction means the fulfilment of their needs. According to the great writer Honoré de Balzac, this has disastrous consequences:

> The first use that Castanier had promised himself that he would make of the terrible power bought at the price of his eternal happiness, was the full and complete indulgence of all his tastes . . . . The devil had given him the key of the storehouse of human pleasures; he had filled and refilled his hands, and he was fast nearing the bottom. In a moment he had felt all that that enormous power could accomplish; in a moment he had exercised it, proved it, wearied of it. What had hitherto been the sum of human desires became as nothing. So often it happens that with possession the vast poetry of desire must end, and the thing possessed is seldom the thing that we dreamed of.

Balzac continues his analysis:

> He took his pleasure like a despot; a blow of the ax felled the tree that he might eat its fruits. The transitions, the alternations that measure joy and pain, and diversify human happiness, no longer existed for him. He had so completely glutted his appetites that pleasure must overpass the limits of pleasure to tickle a palate cloyed

with satiety, and suddenly grown fastidious beyond all
measure, so that ordinary pleasures became distasteful.[1]

Like Castanier before his conversion, many people do not realize that dissatisfaction plays an indispensable role within the very
heart of desire. Practically all psychologists are in agreement that,
depending on how it is recognized and embraced, dissatisfaction
can be a springboard towards a more integrated life. My intention
in this chapter is to underline the importance of dissatisfaction
within religious experience that connects with others and with Jesus, especially thanks to better-centred prayer. We will also see that
dissatisfaction is central to witnessing to the gospel, because being
a Christian is not a matter of moral prowess; rather, it is marked by
authenticity and inauthenticity, success and failure.

A Transition

So long as we imagine that desiring God is a solely positive feeling,
directed at God as to an object, then dissatisfaction will remain
a negative experience. In reality, however, as I will explain in the
next chapter, the profound attraction to God does not consist in
desiring this or that, an object; it is rather a matter of simply desiring. The transition from desiring this or that concrete thing to a
desire that has no particular object allows us to see the true nature
of desire for God. This transition is not accomplished easily, because we have the feeling that we have lost the compass that was
our previous guide. But it is never actually achieved by a person's
efforts alone; it is only to be received as a gift of the Holy Spirit.

This fundamental attitude, however, which consists in desiring pure and simple, must not be confused with an arrogant
wish for enormous appetite, a wish to be a person of desire. In
our day, many people set their sights on being "desire champions,"
as it were, counting themselves as members of an elite group of
people of great passion who succeed in realizing their passions.
An individual may have this debatable ambition, and so too a

1. Balzac, "Melmoth Reconciled."

group of privileged individuals who are puffed up with their superiority. Many people boast of being strongly attached to their passion, which may be something extreme or more of an inoffensive pastime.

As we find in reading Luc Ferry, what we have here is a substitute for Nietzsche's proposition that a successful life is one that is lived with highest intensity.[2] But this substitute leads only to false success:

> Nothing is worse than failure, unless it is success when it is less than total. Nothing is more dangerous than realizing our fantasies. They are not true desires, wishes capable of opening up real possibilities in our lives (of the sort that perhaps should be realized), but indications of an essential frustration that inevitably engenders in us the absurd logic of consumption and a senseless surrender to the universe of merchandise and all its fetishes.[3]

On the other hand, the basic desire that I am describing promotes freedom from all disparate temptations. Yet this freedom is not divorced from sensation: the particular enticements are still in play, but by being grounded in the deep desire that unifies the person, they are relativized in a fundamental manner. Gandhi declared: "The man who lives contented in the self through the self will give up all desires, but one can live in such a state only if the desire to become better, to grow spiritually, awakens in him."[4] The atheist humanist André Comte-Sponville is not far from Gandhi in proposing a total abandonment of hope and the embrace of a "despair" that is compatible with pursuing the great ethical values, which he illustrates by citing Stoic, Hindu, and Buddhist texts. I believe that what he rejects is precisely the hope of particular desires.[5]

Françoise Dolto provides this perspective:

---

2. To appreciate the difference between this substitute and Nietzsche's proposition, see Ferry, *What Is the Good Life?*, chapter 6.

3. Ferry, *What Is the Good Life?*, 12.

4. Gandhi, *Bhagavadgita*, 49.

5. See Comte-Sponville, *Traité*, and Comte-Sponville, *Little Book*.

We find real joy is recovering the cohesion of our entire being, the unity—even if passing—around the core of our desire. And this desire develops as a function of our full being as persons, searching for joy in the calm of all that exists rather than the satisfaction of a partial pleasure.[6]

This unifying desire reaches full strength when we calmly accept that nothing can satisfy it. This makes a healthy detachment possible. We renounce, at the moment when particular fears vanish, as if it were the most natural thing to do; we stop being afraid of losing this or that, including our successes; we stop being afraid of dying.

Complementary Opposites

When we take this affective context into account, we readily see that dissatisfaction is indispensable in our search for God. Our feelings of dissatisfaction are endless. Imperfection, distraction, half-hearted engagement, falling out, loss, humiliation, failure, and so on—all of these negative aspects of our lives frequently surface to impede a vigorous desire for God. Thus we may think that there is a dichotomy between sincere connection with God and the experience of dissatisfaction. But this inner opposition disappears as soon as we realize that the desire for God is no different from the dissatisfaction we find in relation to everything that life offers us. Plenitude and dissatisfaction are the two sides of a single reality, of one and the same experience. The desire for fullness or fulfilment is a positive phenomenon in that it is a power, a stirring of the heart, a self-confident hope, an anticipation of total happiness. Dissatisfaction is a negative phenomenon: as the Hindus so frequently repeat, "Not this, not that, not at all." But Saint John of the Cross says, "*Todo y nada*," "Everything and nothing." In the nothing we find All.

6. Dolto, *L'Évangile*, 31.

These opposites complement each other both successively and simultaneously. They are sequential in that sometimes what we feel more strongly is dissatisfaction, while at other times it is fullness. They are simultaneous when peace underlies our dissatisfaction and when some incompleteness remains beneath our sense of fulfilment. What remains then, when everything has already been taken into account, is the feeling that what is most important to us is still sadly lacking.

Influenced by our desires that aim at finite goods, we give up on the idea that desire will find an object that can bring our quest to a happy conclusion. This renunciation is connected to love of life. It allows us to appreciate more highly the simple and true things that life offers us, yet without becoming shackled to them. As one French moralist put it: "The wise can be happy with a bit of nothing whereas nothing can satisfy the foolish. This shows why almost all people are miserable."[7] This nuanced observation should spur us to fight more realistically and more patiently to improve the human condition. The psychoanalyst Antoine Vergote characterizes desire as "an impetus that overwhelms what it overtakes, a drive that aims beyond its specific destination . . . Desire is that inner pulsation of a being that expects never to complete the entire path to the full emergence of its life." He adds that the infinite is "what fills humans without shutting them up in themselves."[8]

Supports

Curiously, desire discovers its joy within itself, right where an inexhaustible Wellspring surges. It is well aware that the love which embraces it is an extraordinary love. Indeed, our nature as beings of desire is given, fully known, and continually willed by the Creator. Desire comes to terms with dissatisfaction because it understands that a nurturing love has placed it within time so that it may grow. This knowledge grounded in faith gives rise to a peace that "I

---

7. Author unknown.

8. See Vergote, *Interprétation*, 151 and 156.

do not give to you as the world gives" (John 14:27), a joy that "no one will take . . . from you" (John 16:22).

In addition to being accepted by God, our profound desire is sustained by the hope of our brothers and sisters who have faith in God. We are part of creation, which "waits with eager longing for the revealing of the children of God," according to Saint Paul; further, "We know that the whole creation has been groaning in labour pains until now" (Rom 8:19, 22). Desire incarnate in concrete beings encourages us and stimulates us. We need to observe this desire in others from time to time, during dialogue or in prayer meetings.

Our desire is shaped by connecting with that of Jesus, who showed a sense of urgency tinged with anguish when he confided to his disciples: "I came to bring fire to the earth, and how I wish it were already kindled! I have a baptism with which to be baptized, and what stress I am under until it is completed!" (Luke 12:49–50). On the evening of his Last Supper with them he said: "I have eagerly desired to eat this Passover with you before I suffer" (Luke 22:15). And what are we to say of his words on the cross, at once so physical and so symbolic: "I am thirsty" (John 19:28)? Further, after encountering the Source of living water, the risen Christ proclaims: "Let anyone who is thirsty come to me, and let the one who believes in me drink. As the scripture has said, 'Out of the believer's heart shall flow rivers of living water'"; and the Evangelist comments: "Now he said this about the Spirit, which believers in him were to receive; for as yet there was no Spirit, because Jesus was not yet glorified" (John 7:37–39).

Prayer expresses humans' desire for God. I have already mentioned communal prayer, with its rich symbols. Personal prayer is another way to enter into the dynamics of desire, to live with our deep desire. Some consider this prayer to be meta-symbolic because it goes beyond all images and all particular thoughts. With the help of one word or a very short phrase, with the rhythm of our breathing, we can achieve a relaxed attentiveness, conscious of God's presence and in our own human openness. Focusing calmly on our own desire, roused by the Holy Spirit, connects us with an immense force. By being centred on the living God, prayerful men and women discover a strength to move mountains (see Matt 17:20).

Ambiguous Witnessing

Both the world and the Church are in great need of finding people who take their deep desire seriously. When we recognize desire as an invaluable gift, as an invitation to enter into the mystery of divine life, it becomes a living denunciation of the idols that surround us: money, health, sexuality, security, talent, success, group bias, etc. These are genuine values, of course, but they become destructive the moment they take top billing. By contrast, when one of these values is partially or totally lacking—whether in marriage, in religious life, or in other human circumstances—faithfulness to interpersonal relationships with God and with others is an opportunity for Christian witnessing.

This witnessing is never pure, however. Even while trying to be faithful to a God who forbids all forms of idolatry, we detect a mixture of authenticity and inauthenticity. Yet the experience of inauthenticity leads readily to despair, because we then have the impression of being not only inadequate but also false. Influenced by psychology, many of us Christians are afraid that falling into idealism or into repression will cause us to be inauthentic. We are not satisfied with mere words; we want to be sincere and to live life concretely. In practice, this means that typically we govern our behaviour according to purely humanist principles.

As a consequence, we diminish the gospel ideal in order to reduce the troubling gap between what it proposes and our own inadequate performance. In so doing, we even think that we have managed to decrease the bitter dissatisfaction that we feel due to this gap. But adopting an infra-Christian humanism is not a solution. Moreover, when left to its own devices, drained of the meaning that the cross and resurrection of Jesus could provide, humanism gives rise to another kind of dissatisfaction. Because they are necessarily limited, human values ultimately fall flat if they are not enlivened by Christianity. Yes, we can hide behind a rhetorical smokescreen—we can extol our unlimited potential, our personal creativity, our courageous uncertainty in times of great change, and so on. But all this merely transforms the values into idols.

A Difficult Tension

The important point is that the wonderful gift of God, as presented in the New Testament and in the lives of the saints, subjects believers to a difficult tension: the tension between the natural and the supernatural. We are offered a limitless love, and this fact heightens our desire for God as inspired by the Holy Spirit. The transformation of desire makes us realize how unable we are to be faithful to the new reality emerging within us. And the dissatisfaction we feel due to this inability is truly distressing. Yet, fundamentally, it is a sign that we really love God. Far from discouraging us, we can take this dissatisfaction as part of the extraordinary gift we receive from Jesus.

To put it somewhat differently: for people who penetrate beyond the perspectives of straightforward humanism, taking the supernatural seriously introduces a properly religious tension. More ambitious than humanism, gospel radicalism puts our weakness on clear display. Our desire becomes stronger at the precise moment when all we accomplish is a perplexing melange of authenticity and inauthenticity.

What does this imply for Christian witnessing? One thing is for sure: such witnessing cannot be a show put on to impress others. This is true even for the lives of the saints; far from conveying a sense of great achievement, they witness instead to the grace of God that triumphs within human desire become very conscious of its sinfulness. No one described this Christian condition better than Saint Paul: "But we have this treasure in clay jars, so that it may be made clear that this extraordinary power belongs to God and does not come from us" (2 Cor 4:7). He even told the same community: "Therefore, to keep me from being too elated, a thorn was given to me in the flesh" (2 Cor 12:7). God reassured him in his anxiety: "My grace is sufficient for you, for power is made perfect in weakness" (2 Cor 12:9).

From a pagan point of view, isn't there something ridiculous and tragic in the intention to build a family, a religious community, or a Christian parish with people of limited gifts, attracted to the idols of society and more than ready to betray their ideals? Aren't we exposing ourselves to mockery if this is the way we make public commitments? Our rejoinder to this objection should not be to renounce the gospel message; rather, it is a matter of accepting weakness as an essential part of the human experience. We Christians are clowns who, with our pretensions deflated, invite the presumptuous and the cynical alike to recognize that there is a profound attitude towards life that goes beyond a manic embrace of idols or a disengaged resignation. We find ourselves here at the heart of the paradox of the cross as described by Paul: "For I think that God has exhibited us apostles as last of all, as though sentenced to death, because we have become a spectacle to the world, to angels and to mortals. We are fools for the sake of Christ" (1 Cor 4:9–10).

Christian witnesses are not afraid of being put on display if they have accepted their deep dissatisfaction as an integral component of God's desire. Notwithstanding the mistakes and shortcomings and the suffering that they cause, life according to the gospel is worth living—with weakness matching strength, with dissatisfaction matching desire—in broad daylight. Far from rejecting the tension created by the supernatural, far from falling back on worldly ways, far from diminishing their desire and making it small, believers allow themselves to be drawn by and towards God. Those who give in to a humanistic outlook hope to benefit from the warmth of the divine fire without truly committing themselves to it. Only those who plumb the depths of their desire accept being burned in it.

8

Desirability

THE FEELING OF DESIRABILITY plays a central part in the psychology of desire. I can think of no better way to describe it than through the thought of Sebastian Moore.[1] I met this English Benedictine at Boston College and we became friends. I will focus on *The Fire and the Rose Are One*, his masterpiece.[2]

Shared Energy

In my opinion, Moore succeeds in his attempt to convey the nuances of human desire. He manages to elucidate a central feature that has been neglected consistently by the modern Western tradition. If asked, "What does it mean to desire someone's presence?" many people would respond: "A person feels this desire when feeling an inner lack, an unsatisfied need, a void to be filled." Few would say: "We desire someone's presence when we experience an inner vitality, an intensity, a feeling of richness to be actualized with another person." And if the question were to be asked, "What does it mean to be good?" many would answer: "Being good consists in

1. See Roy, "Sebastian Moore's Spiritual Vision," 165–77.

2. Moore, *Fire*. A more schematic presentation of these ideas appears in Moore, *Let This Mind*.

not doing harm to others, in satisfying their needs, and in doing good to them." Rarely would one hear: "Being good consists in living well, in letting a love of life shine forth and flourish, and in sharing one's joy, interests, and talents with others."

Now, for Moore, to desire and to do good are not simply equivalent to receiving and giving. They are based fundamentally and above all on one's being in a good state and feeling content to be what one is. In other words, the love one feels for another is neither dearth nor devotion; rather, it requires an appreciation for what one is, what one has, what one could have, and it blossoms in a desire to share. This attention to the psychology of love allows Moore to present, successfully and in a novel manner, the ontological conviction of Aquinas that all being is good and desirable in itself.

Moore's originality consists in articulating this truth from the vantage point of self-awareness. For the human being endowed with intelligence and love, being good means to feel good about oneself in relation to another. Everything truly starts with self-esteem, which shapes relationships with others. On one side, those who lack self-esteem tend to compensate for its absence by looking for gratification ever more frequently, no matter how this might affect others. On the other side, those with self-esteem rejoice in being recognized in the very moment that their actions enrich the lives of others. When the first sort of individual experiences intimacy, the implicit or explicit message to the other person is "I don't amount to very much. But love me and I won't feel so empty." In the other case, the message is "You and I both have personal value. How good it is to be together!"

Moore contends that if there is one feeling for which every human being yearns, it is precisely to feel good with oneself and with others. It is the conviction that one has value, that one is recognized and desired. Being convinced of one's value and desirability opens the door to truly desiring and loving. By contrast, feelings of emptiness or of being undesirable cause a person to be at odds with others, their relationships inevitably flawed. An individual who is deprived of affection either asks very little of others or requests artificial forms of satisfaction from them. Someone who does not feel good either loses appetite or becomes bulimic. The springboard for loving fully is not a negative attitude towards oneself, but one's interest in particular projects, activities, or people—that is, all those things that enrich one's life. And this has nothing to do with feelings of self-sufficiency, with vanity or independence. On the contrary: such attitudes would reveal a deep self-doubt. In reality, those whose own vitality and spontaneity grounds their openness to others are conscious both of their own limitations and of what others bring to them.

Others mediate our feeling of being desirable. To make this point dramatically, Moore explores what transpires when a person is sexually aroused or stimulated by another. If the aroused person is healthy, she is put in touch immediately with all her vital potential. Her complex capacity for relationship is set in motion. Pleasure, arising from some concrete action, initiates a relationship with another. But this phenomenon absolutely does not reduce to genital arousal. This general law highlighted by Moore applies to every form of human connection that inspires and produces an interesting activity. Whoever the parties may be—parents and children, teachers and students, male and female friends, and collaborators of all kinds—as soon as a situation allows someone to unleash their potential, we may say that such an individual is actualizing her love thanks to the confidence—usually implicit—that another person has expressed to her.

There is a duality to this love. It is both love of self and love of the other; it desires the other and it desires the desire within the other. But we must not model this reciprocal desire on biological need for some object. The profound wish of human desire does not consist in wanting to take hold of another; rather, it hopes to kindle the other's desire for me. True joy blossoms when I discover that the other is enlivened, is attracted and feels good in this interpersonal activity. So what one hopes to evoke in the other is not desire-as-need; rather, one wishes to elicit the other's feelings with regard to one's desire and one's desirability. What is truly gratifying is to feel the other's intensity when one is awakened to the highest form of desire—the form in which one shares the best of oneself with another human being.

The author calls this yearning "the desire to be oneself for another." "Being for" means both to give oneself and to be recognized simultaneously. We should appreciate the extent to which, for Moore, true affection is neither egocentric nor heterocentric; instead, it dynamically engages two fundamental desires. Consciousness of self and others and love of oneself and others interact naturally and support each other. The aberrations of narcissism do not lead the author to discount love of self. Instead, he considers it necessary to delve into the essential wish that underlies narcissism: the wish of a person to be persuaded that he is important in the eyes of another. This is the one and only path that leads to mutuality, to attitudes that favour the happiness of the other, to the capacity to accept confrontation and to grow through it. Affirmation of the self and affirmation of the other are two sides of a single reality.

The Question and the Experience of God

Many contemporary thinkers help us to identify the forms of the question of God in our day. Moore's approach is to help us to address this question at the heart of our most central concern: ourselves. In the opening chapters of *The Fire and the Rose Are One*, he begins by showing that happiness does not consist in the absence of irritants but in the consciousness individuals have of their personal value. As we have seen, he then declares that the deepest desire is to be someone for somebody else; and great joy surges naturally when the other person responds to this expectation.

We may well wonder occasionally about the source and meaning of such desire and experience when they appear from time to time with so much intensity. "Why in fact do I exist as a being-of-desire?" is a question that highlights the problem of my own worth as a human being. Moore poses the question of God here in a most engaging manner. Within a perspective that starts with human affectivity, he wishes to complete a metaphysical account of the source and meaning of all that exists. Although it has undeniable intellectual validity, the metaphysical approach generally goes no-where unless the same question is posed simultaneously from a psychological viewpoint. Philosophical considerations of all that is real come across as too cold, too huge, even soul-crushing to souls in search of meaning that can engage them existentially. Moore allows room for philosophical considerations, but briefly and at a second stage where we confirm rationally that the God understood in terms of desire is not an illusion but corresponds effectively to the creator of all that exists.

Furthermore, while the metaphysical approach usually gives the appearance of being uncertain and misleading, the psycho-logical approach also has its difficulties. Moore emphasizes the fact that many people refuse to take the question of their own im-portance seriously. They are wary of the exaggeration that comes with narcissism; and they think that believers mistake their desires for reality and create a God from whole cloth who is passionately interested in humanity.

In response to this high-minded objection, Moore under-takes to demonstrate the existence of a human desire for God, for which he marshals a central idea of Ernest Becker.[3] In effect, Moore accepts Becker's thesis that contrasts an individual's need to safeguard her personal value with how she confronts the inescap-able fact of her death. Becker holds that the denial of death consists in refusing to be dominated by a troubling mystery: I did not al-ways exist and one day I will leave this world. Because this inescap-able fact mocks the instinct for self-preservation of (in Becker's terms) the "human animal," we repress our awareness of this truth; we deny our dependent state and affirm our autonomy; we strive to construct a self through our undertakings in order to prove to ourselves that we are important and to give meaning to our lives.

Moore accepts Becker's position on the denial of death, and he does not regard as futile the search for personal value that is manifested in this denial. Moore knows full well that, during this short earthly life, a person can dismiss the troubling mystery of the void from which he came and to which he will return. However, he

3. Becker, *Denial of Death.*

can ask: "What if the meaning and fulfilment of my impassioned interest in myself lie in the discovery that I am important for that mystery from which I have my origin?"

This question shows the difference between Ernest Becker and Moore. Becker falls into the common contradiction of talking *intelligently* about life being ultimately *absurd*; whereas Moore asserts that the pursuit of meaning to its terminus supposes acceptance of the ultimate purpose of the fundamental desire that constitutes the uniqueness of human beings. As Moore explains, Becker thought that the human animal's pursuit of meaning requires humans to reject the idea of dependency in regard to a troubling mystery. It did not occur to Becker that this mystery could be anything other than a threat to the tentative and precarious security of the self. By contrast, Moore finds this much-sought meaning in precisely that dependency upon the mystery. But to make it possible to accept that dependence, Moore probes honestly into how the mystery may be characterized.

He comes to this by returning to the analysis of desire and by finding in it a depth that allows us to talk about God in a manner that is as rationally rigorous as it is emotionally rich. In effect, as I said earlier, it has to do with demonstrating the existence of a human desire for God. At the beginning of his work *The Inner Loneliness*,[4] he focuses on the paradox of inner solitude: the very thing within me that drives me to enter into relationship seems fated never to be shared. No one could ever experience the feeling that I have of being special, unique, and priceless in exactly the way that I feel it from the inside. Now this conviction—my conviction that, albeit being aware of my limitations, I am a being of irreplaceable value in spite of everything—may actually have a real foundation. Moore draws attention to the indignation and anger that overcome those who feel neglected, abandoned, discredited, or despised. If the feeling that every human being shares of his worth is an illusion, how can we explain the fully spontaneous impression that the denial of this worth is something unjust and unacceptable?

4. Moore, *Inner Loneliness*.

Yet if this feeling, on the one hand, is not an illusion, and if no one else can share it fully, on the other, are we not here in the presence of a human desire for God? Is there not a wish in the innermost depth of the human heart—a hesitant but no less real yearning—to be completely understood and loved for the treasure within us that we consider most precious, namely our desirability? Doubtless this desire remains unformulated most of the time. However, it must not be thought of as a substitute for desire between humans. On the contrary: when it is lived well, the desire for God augments the quality and intensity of interpersonal relationships.

The Awareness of Being Desirable

Moore spells out the two faces of desire—desire between humans and desire for God—as follows. To begin, let us recall what we have already seen with respect to the inter-human face of desire. The desire at play in my experience of being attracted to a person, a value, or an activity has a source, namely the feeling of being desirable that awakens and intensifies through the mediation of what attracts me. So we have three terms here:

1. That which is desired
2. The fact of desiring
3. My desirability

What is desired, namely the person or value or activity that I pursue (1), is the intermediary arriving from outside me to cause me to desire (2) and to arouse my desirability (3). What is desired (1) activates the potential of well-being, of self-worth and esteem from others (3) which brings about the fact that I desire, the fact of desiring (2).

What, then, is the other face of desire, relative to this tripartite schema? What is at play is a desire without a particular object, which many people feel without appreciating its full import. In this instance, the first term—what is desired—is absent. The experience consists in *just wanting* (2), in having an immediate sense of one's desirability (3), in feeling content about desiring without desiring anything in particular. With regards to the inter-human face of desire, I grasp my own desirability *indirectly* thanks to the mediation of what I desire (or, more intensely, of the person I desire). With regards to the divine–human face of this selfsame desire, I grasp my own desirability *directly*—as activated within me, without any intermediary. Such is the philosophical structure of the emotional experience of God.

It can be relatively easy for some people to identify the incomparable Being who awakens and confirms our true desirability from within ourselves. Generally, however, our openness to God is marked by feelings of ambivalence. Moore tells us that we can be profoundly in love with the Source of our existence while simultaneously harbouring a certain hostility towards it. On account of all the evil here on earth that compromises our real desirability, it is quite normal, during our religious journey, to feel divided within ourselves with regards to the Creator. Moore shed light on this path by distinguishing two major phases. In a first phase, a person longs for the Being who would confirm her worth definitively. Then, in a second phase, she mysteriously hears the response that she hoped for but did not dare to hope for. I believe that the ineffable meaning and joy felt in this second phase go far towards reducing the ambivalence and intensifying the positive feelings towards God.

So we see that Moore sheds a highly original light on the question and experience of God. As opposed to many Christian thinkers who do not go far enough in their exploration of desire, Moore does not stop at saying that the encounter with God resembles an interpersonal encounter. When they fix on this parallel, these writers do not show *how* approaching and discovering God produce an overabundance of meaning and joy—and in fact, a fullness of meaning and joy that cannot be found in human relationships. By demarcating the question of God and by showing how our feeling of desirability depends upon the experience of God, Moore renders inestimable service to religious psychology and to theology.

9

Liberation of Desire

MY FIRST CHAPTER PRESENTED a quick overview of human autonomy, based on a spontaneous quest of individuals for freedom in relation to their drives and to other persons. Even though the child begins life completely dependent upon his parents and then on other members of society, it is normal for him to gain autonomy bit by bit and then affirm it increasingly in adolescence. Nevertheless, every lucid and honest individual will admit that a particular confusion colours his search for freedom. He will surely acknowledge that his desire reaches a dead end: holding onto what is clearly unsuitable, arrogant displays of superiority, servile demonstrations of inferiority, unreasonable rivalry, violence, envy, jealousy, deviousness, and so on. An individual will say that his freedom is sometimes a clumsy thing, its own source of failure, at least partially. So he learns painfully to manage his personal and interpersonal crises.

Thus the simple desire for freedom engenders a further desire, the desire to be freed. I will continue to make use of the thought of Sebastian Moore to explore the liberation that allows for the growth of healthy relationships.

Two Forms of Guilt

The more that a person finds her desire to be rewarding, the more she grasps its meaning, scope, and limits. Someone who loves learns more about love than someone who does not love. But rarely do the absolute extremes apply in these matters—no one lives exclusively in light or in shadow. We cannot help being struck by the mix of clarity and muddle in which we find ourselves when it comes to those singular realities of desire, love, and human relationships. And it is here that Christianity has something unique to offer, thanks to its long preoccupation with the challenges of love and equally with the problem of evil. In order to make a meaningful contribution to Christian beliefs in this area, Moore takes the findings of psychoanalysis on the subject of guilt for his starting point; but his philosophy of desire allows him to be creative and to propose clarifications that go beyond Freud's discoveries.

The phenomenological record shows that the opposite of loving oneself is the shame the self feels when it swells up and demands attention. It feels momentary exaltation, even euphoria; but self-deceit soon leads to discontent and depression. Now while many Christian thinkers decried this self-importance without understanding it, Moore interprets this recurring cycle of euphoria and depression as a problem in the love of a self that is maladjusted, uncertain of itself, trying feebly to find itself. Within this clumsy self-affirmation Moore discerns a lack of self-confidence and even a self-hatred that propels this search for love into a series of dead ends. His diagnosis concludes that, far from being excessive self-love, this shows an actual dearth of love of self. He rightly considers this deficiency to be the main reason for the moral predicaments caused by individuals who lack love. Because they do not respect themselves as much as the Creator respects them, because they denigrate themselves overtly or secretly, such people lack the courage to invest the best of themselves in their relationships with others. Instead, they pursue all sorts of superficial and negative whimsies.

Moore notes that humans are curiously resistant to their true desirability. In part, this resistance comes from the guilt that a person inevitably feels in his experience of being free. His own wishes were generally subordinated to those of adults when he was a child; when giving in, he often repressed his love for himself. Thus conflict arose between the expression and the control of his desire. Learning self-control allowed him to avoid the opposition of adults and kept him safe. From then on, whenever he affirms his desire in a manner that does not conform to the expectations of those around him, he feels guilty. As Erich Fromm explains, guilt appears as soon as an individual leaves his environment and acts independently.[1] Even if his behaviour is morally irreproachable, he will feel that he is at fault in relation to the family or societal norms that he defies. This facet of guilt is different from moral failure; it is the feeling that attaches to the idea of doing as one pleases, of going one's own way, of thinking and deciding for oneself rather than sticking to traditional wisdom absorbed during the years of socialization.

This first form of guilt—Moore calls it infantile guilt—remains long after childhood, if not for the whole of a person's life. Nevertheless, it is not the most important form. A second form of guilt does indeed exist. Called "adult guilt" by Moore, it is not to be understood in relation to affirmation of freedom but in relation to the relational character of human beings. It is the feeling that results from having failed another person, from not having given her due, from not having responded to her call or her love. This feeling goes hand in glove with that of having failed oneself; that is, of having betrayed one's inner wish to be in relationship and to share. The evil thus committed—or the sin, to use religious language—does not consist solely in wrong done to another. It is something more radical: the fact of a person making peace with the part of herself that is afraid to love, the fact that she cuts off the source of life that could have flowed from her towards another. When a person commits evil, she inflicts harm on herself as much as on others. This is the most lamentable misunderstanding that

---

1. Fromm, *Man for Himself.*

could possibly occur: the renunciation of one's own profound self and preference for a superficial self that seeks control and power, and flees from authentic human relationships.

Sonia, a character in Dostoyevsky's great novel *Crime and Punishment*, listens to Raskolnikov confess his crime. She cries out: "What, what have you done to yourself!" And she sobs in utmost compassion: "No one, no one in the whole world, is unhappier than you are now!" Later on in this most harrowing of conversations, Raskolnikov declares: "Was it the old crone I killed? I killed myself, not the old crone!"[2]

What confronts us here is an abominable act, the murder of two women. And yet, the same type of deficiency can be present without it causing grievous external evil. All it requires is for a person to suppress a certain capacity in himself to listen, to react with generosity, to act with sincere interiority. Moore notes that this suppression is largely unconscious; and simply overlooking this part of oneself weakens it and, over time, does it serious injury. We sometimes say of a person that "He is heartless." This often implies a hardness of heart, but the phrase applies just as well to someone who anaesthetizes his heart, who tries to neutralize it. Such an individual is actually the first victim of his unfortunate orientation. And his victimhood is all the deeper because he can never fully eliminate his desire to love and be loved. This is truly a case of a wounded and wounding heart.

Accordingly, sin consists in ratifying our tendency to flee from authentic, engaged relationships with others. But where does this tendency come from? To answer this question, Moore draws first on genetic psychology and then on the Judeo-Christian doctrine of original sin.

He begins by describing the two principal crises for the personality of the child. Margaret Mahler shows how deeply decisive is the first crisis, which covers mainly the first two years of life.[3] In effect, the infant must learn to deal with her own individuality. Maybe her mother gives her an ambiguous message that makes

2. Dostoyevsky, *Crime and Punishment*, 411, 412, and 420.

3. Mahler et al., *Psychological Birth*.

her anxious: "Stay a part of me or rely on yourself alone!" Because parents are never perfectly clear, it is impossible for a child to always receive exactly the right amount of support and of encouragement to allow her to develop her individuality in a harmonious manner. The second crisis—the Oedipal crisis brought to light by Freud—is well known. Coming later than the first, it completes the separation of the girl or boy from the parent of the opposite sex. Once again, children must contain their desire, which becomes the id; they must accept a self that is shaped by the roles appropriate to their sex; and finally they must deal with the superego (Freud's Über-Ich, the "above me") constituted by the parent of the same sex, who confirms that complete intimacy with the parent of the other sex is forbidden.

What is the most important consequence of these two crises? According to Mahler, while the child tends spontaneously to love everything that exists, in the course of growing up he learns to control and even repress this love. The constraints imposed on him lead him to doubt his desirability. The impediments imposed on him drive him to hate his desire, condemning it for putting him in situations where he suffers. Thinking that it is self-love that drives him to seek what is bad for him, he learns to mistrust such tendencies and he feels guilty for loving himself. Taken to the extreme, where circumstances have been particularly hard, he feels hatred and disgust for what is best in him: his capacity to love, to be loved, and to enjoy this love. This is the process that leads children to violate their own desirability.

Sin as a Failure of Desire

To recapitulate: the first form of guilt arises from the emergence of the self, the individuality that detaches originally from the mother's breast and then from the familial and societal milieu. Called "infantile" by Moore—I am inclined to add "and adolescent"—this guilt can release a wish to affirm one's autonomy in a way that does not respect others. There is sin in this case to the extent that this sort of self-affirmation, which hurts others, is at play.

The second and "adult" form of guilt draws us still deeper into the heart of the human drama. It arises when an opportunity to love is shut off; it wells up when an offer of interpersonal relationship, that is worthy of beginning or developing, earns a non-response or an inadequate response. Here, too, there is no sin unless the non-response is voluntary.

It might be asked how such a non-response could be voluntary and free. I believe that we have to affirm this fact even if we admit that we cannot understand the raison d'être for the sin. In effect, the sin is precisely that which has no raison d'être, no reason to be. Although explanations can be found for this aberrant behaviour, the decision itself which constitutes the sin remains unintelligible, irrational. Following Thomas Aquinas[4] and Bernard Lonergan,[5] Moore emphasizes the absurdity of sin: it rejects what is good, it prefers non-value over a value that is worthy of existing, it denies what God would wish to create through us. What a mysterious prerogative of human beings—free to both love and not love!

Moore also examines original sin. In his reading of the third chapter of Genesis, he does not accept a widespread interpretation according to which, after the separation from God, the first revolt against the spirit was sexual. On the contrary, he says, it is the spirit that began to mistrust sexuality. "Then the eyes of both were opened, and they knew that they were naked; and they sewed fig leaves together and made loincloths for themselves" (Gen 3:7). The shame that made them cover themselves consists in awareness within human intelligence that became confused after the rupture with the Source of intelligibility. In other words, the self that affirmed itself in opposition to God turns to affirming itself against its own sexuality, the locus par excellence of desire. Only then does desire retaliate against a self that no longer welcomes it.

At this point in his thought, Moore becomes prophetic. He denounces a major Western current that has been highly influential both within and outside Christianity. He calls it "the voice of

4. See Aquinas, *Summa Theologiae*, I-II, q. 71, a. 6, ad 5: sin is counter to reason (*contra rationem*).

5. Lonergan, *Insight*, 689–91.

sin." This is the voice of the sinful self, which takes issue both with God and with sexuality. This voice declares: "Life and death teach me that I should not take my desires for reality. Reality, which I am forced to accept, is limited to what I can acquire through control of myself and others here below (and some might add: in the beyond)." This voice belongs to the self that repels its desire and refuses to be open to its deeper level of self.

Here Moore employs Jung's distinction between the *ego* and the *self*. To put it into non-technical language, let us say that a person's *ego* corresponds to her personality, with well-defined boundaries and traits, which guides her actions and shapes her destiny. As for the *self*, it corresponds to a larger zone that surrounds the ego and to which the ego can gain access if it allows itself to be drawn in, in an unnerving manner, by more powerful forces than the ego. Then, in line with Moore's definition of these two terms, the voice of sin is that of the ego when it opposes the self. When it suppresses sexuality, not only is sexuality crushed as a symbol of desire; worse, it crushes desire itself, which by its nature is open to God.

This rejection of desire is the situation of many, of believers as much as non-believers. For all those who opt for an ego that is cut off from their deepest desire, the voice of sin tells them to resign themselves to a "reality" seen in the perspective of control and power. In this connection, the staggering discovery to which Moore leads us is that in the witnessing and discourse of many Christians, the voice of sin conceals itself within the doctrine of original sin. And whereas this doctrine, which in itself is true, points to the alienating state from which God wishes us to escape, the voice of sin takes it captive and declares: "You can never reach a culmination of your desire. But force yourself to restrain desire, and in so doing you will merit eternal life."

Considered in relation to our earthly existence, this is clearly the voice of hopelessness. It does not take the grace of the Holy Spirit seriously; nor the Father's resolve in favour of salvation; nor the resurrection of Jesus and its decisive character since his life on earth, which is affirmed by the entire New Testament—even if their effects remain incomplete. In fact, this voice negates the propulsive liberation of desire that could begin right away. Thus, according to whether it is authentic or inauthentic, Christianity listens to the voice of the Holy Spirit or to the voice of sin. To the extent that Christianity has listened to the voice of the ego closed in on itself, it has simply reflected the masculine culture of modern times, simultaneously disregarding nature, desire, and the feminine.

It is clear that Moore's conception of desire is utterly opposed to the narrow conception that is dominant in the West. For him, desire, just like intelligence, consists in an essentially open dynamic—or intentionality, as some contemporary philosophers would say. However, this intentionality can become limited artificially due to widespread prejudices. We have noted Moore's presentation of the ramifications of this improper limitation of desire, as much psychological as religious. What is more remarkable is the link he has found between the non-openness of desire and non-openness towards God. When we refuse the consequences of a desire that penetrates to its own greatest depth, for calamitous psychological reasons, we reject the call of that Fullness that makes itself heard in the heart of our desire. Not wanting to die, the ego refuses to transform into a much larger self. The original sin consists in refusing the risks of desirability, and consequently shutting itself off from the true God.

The Freedom that Jesus Offers

Sebastian Moore has always been fascinated by Jesus. All his life he has tried to take the salvation offered by Jesus Christ seriously, wondering how to speak of it without wallowing in verbosity. The inspiration came to him in a country church near Rome, during the Feast of the Sacred Heart, at the moment when the first antiphon of Vespers was being chanted: "Instead, one of the soldiers pierced his side with a spear, and at once blood and water came out" (John 19:34). Moore comments: "Quietly, and with a part of the mind that does not wrestle with concepts, I knew that the whole thing was there: the act of aggression, of sin, releasing the waters of grace."[6]

The whole thing was indeed there, in that richly fertile vision, but in order to draw out its real significance, it was necessary to relate it to central aspects of lived experience. So when Moore thinks about Jesus, he focuses upon a sphere or locus of interaction between Jesus and every person who is interested in him. What might this be? It is the fundamental human experience of being faced with the challenge of clarifying and transforming who one is upon contact with Jesus. This is why what Moore says about desire is so important—especially about desirability, about the question and experience of God, about guilt and about sin. We can look upon Moore's reflections as a creative transposition for our times of the modes of interaction between Christ and a meditator developed by Ignatius of Loyola in the cultural context of the sixteenth century. In fact, the thirty days of the Spiritual Exercises done in 1971 proved to be a turning point in Moore's life.

Moore gives us an original approach to the event of Jesus Christ. Considering the life and death of Jesus, he distinguishes the perspective of Christ's adversaries from that of his disciples. The former managed to liquidate him: why? The current explanation is that Jesus had become a threat to the politico-religious establishment of Jerusalem. Moore certainly does not deny this real factor. But his psychological hypothesis leads him to excavate to a more radical level of understanding, which shines a light on our own attitudes as readers.

If the authorities of that time attacked Jesus, it was because they had discovered, and they feared and loathed, the exceptional human quality of Jesus. This is the sort of quality that contrasts with everyday dreariness and accentuates the sense one has of barely living. People discerned in Jesus a heart full of love and generosity that they had repressed, not without pain, in themselves. For these people who were subject to a rigid, rules-riddled socio-religious regime, it felt like a reproach to meet a prophet who lived his desirability to its fullest, in constant relationship with a fatherly and

6. Moore, *Crucified Jesus*, ix.

compassionate God. Some of Israel's leaders slipped into a dangerous resentment of Jesus—the sort of mute hostility that wells up
when people are faced with the goodness and nobility of someone
better than themselves. Those who had given in to sin, to infantile guilt, and to death, and had hidden this surrender under the
cloak of a literal faithfulness to the law of God, could not accept
the liberating message of Jesus. In the words of the mouthpiece of
the great Russian thinker Soloviev in one of his dialogues: "Alas, a
corrupted heart cannot abide it when good responds to evil. Noble
spirits disturb mediocrity, the light frightens darkness."[7]

In spite of its destructiveness, the attitude of the enemies of Jesus remains superficial because it is bound to a vague appreciation
of desire, guilt, and sin. In contrast, the disciples who witnessed
the preaching of Jesus found their consciousness of these realities
heightened to the extreme by the fact that they were living with
a master with uninhibited desire—the Father's beloved, guiltless
and sinless. Thanks to Jesus, in Galilee they discovered both their
desirability and the love of God with an incomparable intensity.
Through Jesus as intermediary, who brought their desire to a peak
that cannot be described, they had the most profound experience
of God, who increased their hope enormously. And yet this hope
was dashed, as the disciples on the road to Emmaus show us (Luke
24:19–21). The voice of sin made itself heard in the brutal end
of Jesus, and it appeared to be final. So sin, guilt, isolation, and
death triumphed over love, meaning, and desire! And where Jesus
himself failed, no one else could succeed. With Jesus gone, there
was no further reason to hope. On Good Friday, the disciples were
utterly broken, shattered.

Moore emphasizes forcefully that through Jesus, the disciples
experienced an ultimate defeat of mediation towards God—but
this must be viewed in relation to the fact that one can be awakened to one's true desirability by an exterior or an interior process.
With the living Jesus, the disciples approached their desirability
from the outside, being brought to it by friendship with Jesus. However, Moore interprets the presence of the risen Christ as calling

7. Soloviev, *Trois entretiens*, 153.

the disciples *from the inside* to recover their desirability, lost when Jesus was defeated and put to death. Since God alone can thus raise someone to his true, loving vitality without any intermediary, Moore points out that in doing this, Jesus performs a properly divine function; and at the experiential level, the appearances of Jesus are the first steps towards recognition of his divinity.

In this encounter with the risen Christ, believers have an experience of God that completely integrates those facets of evil that are death, sin, and guilt. It may be that the presence of Jesus alive after his death cannot be significantly different from the experience of God without reference to Jesus that is covered in the preceding chapter, because they both involve the action of the Holy Spirit in the human heart. Nevertheless, the encounter with Jesus Christ is more complete than the pre-Christian experience of God because no dimension of the human condition is excluded. Truly, this alone is capable of showing how far the negation of self and others can go: as far as attacking the life of God offered in Jesus. Nowhere is the brutal power of sin so evident as in the sight of the righteous condemned, the innocent victim, the sacrificial lamb.

At the same time, through the resurrection of Jesus—that is, through a purely divine reversal of the situation that is beyond our comprehension—the cross of Jesus becomes an occasion of repentance. In Moore's view, the feeling that the crucifixion should arouse is less one of guilt (a global sense of being at fault) or regret (remorse after something happens that should have gone differently) than of sadness, of sorrow. Sorrow is felt due to the discovery that the interpersonal relationship itself (and not this or that particular act) is amiss. The wounded and wounding heart realizes that it has wounded itself and wounded God in wounding others. When the sorrow connects with this salutary realization, it opens those who experience it to the possibility of a new relationship with another. And when this other who pardons is the resurrected Jesus, a unique quality of hope is offered.

Guilt loses its power when brought before God who casts away our sin through the man Jesus and restores our desirability. More precisely, what fades away is the guilt nourished by sin, which consists in rejecting our own desirability and that of God, and casts a shadow over God, creating a darkened and angry God. But the impact of the resurrection is this: that the Holy Spirit invites us to allow ourselves to live again, to go beyond the limits of the self, to recognize that the love manifested by the life, death, and appearances of Jesus can recreate our desire, open it totally to the divine plan, and engage it in establishing more humanizing social relationships and structures.

10

Spiritual Accompaniment

THIS CHAPTER PRESENTS PATHS of spiritual accompaniment,[1] with Sebastian Moore's thought as touchstone once again. Readers will find some repetition of points from the previous chapter; these are required in order to make sense of the highly original notion of accompaniment that arises from Moore's intuitions.

Love and Desire

Human desire invigorated by the Holy Spirit is the principal dynamism of spiritual life. We have already seen that Moore distinguishes between two kinds of desire. First there is desire-as-need that takes possession of things that satisfy hunger, thirst, and natural necessities. The second is a deeper, specifically human desire: the desire for interpersonal presence in which each partner feels well-being with the other and within himself or herself. It is easier to have an image of the first desire than the second, the latter being more complex and more difficult to depict. This is why it is dangerous to describe the second in terms of the first. If we fall into this trap, we reduce love to a transaction in which something is offered

1. The *accompaniment* referred to occurs typically in group or individual retreats or in psychological counselling sessions. (Translator's note)

or taken. Setting up a contrast between these two sorts of interaction leads to the false opposition between altruism and egoism; moreover, it heightens the inner malaise of those who only do one of the two, giving or receiving. Another ploy might have us try to reduce this tension by means of a compromise in which altruism and egoism simply take turns.[2]

The problem persists so long as we fail to perceive—across every sort of relationship—the deep yearning of our desire that is fixed upon experiencing our own and the other's well-being in what we are and in what we live through together. Great joy flows from this experience, which provides the fullest possible meaning to the satisfaction of giving and receiving. This mutual attention unites two people at a higher level than that of need-desire, which is based on what is exchanged. Desire at this higher level is realized in the close connection between love for the other and love of self. And this desire is the source of all human validation. It reveals its unique richness, on which we can build in order to grow. It does not start from a feeling of emptiness, patterned on experiences of hunger, thirst, and other biological needs. On the contrary, it springs from a zest for life that seeks to share its presence.

In our relating to God, it is also in the realm of fundamental desire—not in need-desire—that the relationship is initiated and enhanced. When this relationship seems to be discordant, even alienating, the reason is that we see things through the lens of desire as need; and we have very little confidence in our personal capacity to live deep desire. In these circumstances, the required spiritual accompaniment should help an individual to clarify her horizontal connections with others. Has she ever been conscious, even at an inchoate level, of experiencing a mutual presence that gave rise to joy and appreciation? If there is even just a bit of experience of this sort, it can be used to shine light on the vertical relationship with God.

Nevertheless, Moore notes that any analogy between a human relationship and the relationship with God is inadequate. An experience *of God* is essential to buttress supernatural life. What

2. Concerning egoism and altruism see Roy, *Self-Actualization.*

does this imply? It means that, albeit the parallel between human love and the love that unites one with God, there is also a major difference. In human love, I am awakened to my true value when I perceive the desire and well-being of the other who is with me; I am thus awakened *from the outside* by the person who interests me. In the encounter with God, the believer is awakened *from the inside*; indeed, it is the Creator who gives me the capacity to desire, the desire itself, and the joy that comes with living a certain fullness. Even though horizontal relationships have prepared the way, this strictly vertical discovery produces a superior light and happiness. It is important, therefore, that the spiritual accompaniment address both aspects: firming up the foundation of love at the human level, and finding the authentically religious foundation that underpins love at the religious level.

Ambivalence and Guilt

Moore shows that a person may well be attracted to God and harbour negative feelings towards God at the same time. The origins of this ambivalence lie in the first years of life with the fact that, necessarily, the child is partly satisfied and partly frustrated by his parents. Human beings come into a finite world, so it is normal for the experience of limits and of evil to nourish ambivalent feelings towards God. Moreover, this confrontation with finitude, which is difficult enough in itself, is further complicated by the addition of another factor: guilt. As the previous chapter recounted, guilt for Moore comes in two forms, infantile and adult. In this section, we will recall how such matters are experienced; in the next, we will focus on the implications for spiritual accompaniment.

When a child is frustrated, she might express her discontent or anger in an entirely spontaneous manner. On the other hand, requiring the goodwill and support of her parents, she might go along with their expectations and wishes. In doing so, she learns to think of whatever impels her to oppose the rules taught by her parents as dangerous and reprehensible. This is the source of *infantile* guilt. It should be emphasized that this form of guilt persists in the adolescent to varying degrees, and even in adults in their adolescent traits. This is the sort of guilt that is displayed when an adult diverges from his group's norms, and especially if he affirms himself in an aggressive manner. He feels guilty for deviating from these norms due to thinking independently; he feels guilty for trying to be himself and to live!

Infantile guilt is ambiguous. On the one hand, it provides either a security barrier for unreflective people or an opportunity for reflection for those who are concerned with acting morally. In this case, the superego helps the ego to develop its moral sense. On the other hand, since infantile guilt is a painful feeling for those who question the rules of the group, it incites them to flee. So as to avoid this accusation, so disagreeable to hear, many people are prepared to allow themselves to be imprisoned in conformity. Even worse, this infantile guilt can lead to destroying desire, or at the very least of neutralizing it. Indeed, in order to escape this guilt, it is tempting to reconcile one's desire with "reality," that is, with the world as defined by those whose authority one accepts. This all leads to an individual banishing, or at least weakening, what she perceives within herself as causing her to revolt against "reality." The inability to endure her infantile guilt leads her to separate from the best part of her desire.

Whereas infantile guilt coincides with self-affirmation with regard to the laws of the family or group, *adult* guilt goes with an appropriate evaluation of interpersonal relationships. Facing the fact that something ought to have taken place but did not—when feelings or values are at issue, or a particular act—the guilt felt by the intelligent heart is deeper than guilt for transgression of a norm. This could be due to regret for having failed someone, of not having offered the respect and love deserved by another person. It could also be regret for having fallen short with respect to one's own conscience—that is, for failing oneself—and not allowing the best part of oneself to blossom and to encounter another individual or group with authenticity.

Such an impasse in a human relationship ought to cause adult guilt to well up. Unfortunately, this is often not the case; and the impasse may worsen further with what Moore sees as the hidden influence of infantile guilt. Recall that to be released from infantile guilt, the natural reaction is to diminish the desire that appears to be responsible for the maladroit ego-affirmation that unleashed the guilt. Yet constricting desire deprives the self of the very resources it needs in order to establish meaningful interpersonal relationships. In anaesthetizing the part of himself that incites him to challenge the principles of the group, the individual is preparing himself to be thwarted in love. Because he has learned to mistrust his desire, he will not have the confidence needed to engage in a relationship that is enriching and therefore demanding as well.

Recognizing Sin

In spiritual accompaniment, the director will first help the person to distinguish the two sorts of guilt within herself. In matters of infantile guilt, the simple fact of bringing her ambiguity to light opens a space of freedom. In discovering that what has caused the guilt is not necessarily that she did something bad, she becomes capable of morally good actions, which nevertheless give rise to infantile guilt because they transgress established standards. One learns therefore to coexist with this guilt. And because this is no longer accepted unconditionally by a person's intelligence, healing can begin: she feels less guilt on account of attitudes and actions that were previously prohibited but are judged henceforth to be morally good. Thus she dissociates herself from her superego and disengages from individuals who reinforced that superego.

Once a person has put some distance between himself and his infantile guilt, he is better able to deal with his adult guilt. Not as close to the surface as the first, the second form is in danger of not being noticed at all. And whereas there is always an ambiguity to infantile guilt, it is a noble thing to accept one's adult guilt. Indeed, this acceptance—to acknowledge one's sin—consists in being truthful (see John 3:19–21 and 1 John 1:6–9). Accordingly, sin does not come from contravening a law; rather, it exists because a value that deserved to be actualized was left unrealized. Due to this omission, a person fails others, himself, and God. By not living what ought to have been lived, he impoverishes the other as much as his own self; and by the same stroke, he has prevented the creative goodness of God from flowing in us.

The accompaniment should help a person to take her sins seriously. Examination of conscience is done more easily if infantile guilt is not front and centre. This guilt, tied to the superego, is truly very far from being a certain guide to the morality of our actions. This is why an exchange with someone to provide guidance is desirable in order to bring the other form of guilt, the adult version, to the fore—the guilt that is based on a rational assessment of one's actions. The first task could be to point out what the person herself misses by sinning. But what should be emphasized above all is sincere, intelligent remorse coming from the bottom of her heart. She feels pain, a regret tied inseparably to the esteem and affection she has for the other. But if pardon is present where this regret is felt, she does not have a reflex to become utterly negative about herself. When this is the case, she may realize that God has not stopped loving her and being present to her throughout her journey. She thinks of Jesus who raises the fallen with warmth, humour, and grace.

When spiritual accompaniment is difficult, it is because the one who is being helped fears the very idea of permitting himself to be loved. I am frightened because my desire leads me into social transgression and causes infantile guilt. I mistrust that part of myself that allows itself to dream and to risk painful disappointments. I do not want to see myself as someone special. In practical terms, what I do is deny my importance as a person, and I renounce much of my hopefulness.

Even though this position is fundamentally opposed to the gospel, religion is often used to justify it. Beneath this wish to not tell big stories about oneself, do we not find a stoical acceptance of an arbitrarily limited "reality"? What is really important here is that this pseudo-realism is an excuse for denying our real sin. Feeling threatened by authentic interpersonal encounters, whether with others or with God, we prefer to retreat into infantile guilt—by accepting it, or by calmly repressing it, or by revolting against it. By this ruse we ignore our adult guilt; or if we become vaguely aware of it, it gives the false impression of being a variant of infantile guilt.

Given that all of this is only obscurely conscious, accompaniment must aim to clarify it. There is a lying inner language, that of sin, that must be heard and decoded. A guide who invites individuals to discern this rationalizing voice inevitably provokes strong objections from some of them. We witness then the battle of the Holy Spirit against impure thoughts within the human heart. We may recall that the only remedy to be rid of these ideas is prayer and fasting (see Matt 17:21).

Inner Division

It is often difficult to resolve the confusion between the infantile and adult forms of guilt. One must wait for an interior split to develop in the person who harbours this confusion. On the one hand, being the victim of a misunderstanding, she will respond positively to accompaniment that tries to release her by making her distance herself from her infantile guilt. On the other hand, there will be resistance to this accompaniment to the extent that the confusion in play forms part of a defence mechanism that allows her to avoid the intense suffering that she associates with the disclosure of her sin. A limited self, which has not learned to truly love, will not assess its faults where love is concerned in a context of adult guilt, but rather one of infantile guilt.

There are different degrees of confusion between the infantile and adult forms of guilt. If a person manages to realize that this confusion is not simply given as such but has received some sort of approval, it is possible to appeal to his honesty. This will help him, especially if this illumination is welcomed as a grace from God, but it will not be enough. He can be trapped into returning to the refuge of infantile guilt, whereas he ought to devote more attention to adult guilt. So long as fear of feeling guilty dominates, infantile guilt continues to be present. By contrast, when a person recognizes his capacity to reject or accept love, he comes to a crossroads. To reject love, he condemns it as unrealistic; to avoid the suffering that comes with love, he listens to the deceitful voice that urges him to anaesthetize his desire and to reduce his expectations to what an arbitrarily restricted "reality" has to offer.

What of the path of accepting love? Here we encounter a mystery of grace and freedom. People may need encouragement to come close to the point of deciding. Moreover, supplemented by the evidence of others, by reading and by meditating on the Gospels, accompaniment can introduce or restore a craving for a great love. Thus, supported by the experience and faith of their guide, individuals seeking boundless love and a prodigious pardon will stop fleeing from their deepest desire and stop loving themselves badly. They will have the courage to advance confidently into the relational adventure that their Creator and Saviour wishes for them.

Returning to the novel by Dostoyevsky quoted in the previous chapter, recall that it was Sonia's compassion for Raskolnikov that opened his eyes to the evil he had done to himself. And as we read in the Epilogue, he finally admits to himself, after his first year in prison, that he is in love with Sonia. "They were both pale and thin, but in those pale, sick faces there already shone the dawn of a renewed future, of a complete resurrection into a new life. They were resurrected by love."[3] This love gives Raskolnikov enduring hope and begins his process of healing.

Welcoming the Resurrection

Christian salvation is more than victory over sin. It also consists in the progression by which the self becomes completely human by opening itself to ever deeper layers of its being and by receiving the life that God offers so generously. Nevertheless, this progression is also marked by hesitancy, trials, and death. It is summed up in the

3. Dostoyevsky, *Crime and Punishment*, 549.

disciples' experience of Jesus, as interpreted by Sebastian Moore (spelled out in the previous chapter). Let us recall the main points.

The proclamation of the Kingdom and the presence of Jesus in Galilee enormously stimulated the loving potential of his companions. Their desire grew in parallel with God's dream for humanity. When opposition to their Master stiffened and finally vanquished him, their vision was dashed by the brutal and implacable fact of the absolute injustice. Moore sees the explanation for the betrayal of Judas in the bitter disappointment; it shows the frustration and anger of one who thought that Jesus had let him down. After the Crucifixion, the disciples could not hope to live fully any longer. Death had had the final word and it infiltrated their very souls.

By dying successively to provisional forms of self, believers can participate in the experience of the disciples of Jesus. The Galilean phase consists in this opening to a great love that I have already presented. In turn, the Passion and the Cross bespeak the crises undergone by persons who must abandon a given mode of functioning in order to reach up to a new way of being and acting. At stake here is the psycho-spiritual growth that God wishes for them and would have them achieve.

Moore points out that these transitions are not easy to achieve because they cause the self to feel insecure and they take it by surprise. Indeed, they cannot be programmed or controlled. Then he goes further and writes that following Jesus in his defeat involves passing beyond death and being brought to perceive, from that point of view, the artificial limits that the self imposes upon itself. Accordingly, with Jesus and his disciples, we gain a sense of life that includes finitude, evil, and death. The Resurrection is the gift of divine life that causes light and life to blossom within the believer, who is thus allowed to truly believe in a greater meaning of life that surpasses the usual ways that "reality" is defined.

Accompaniment stands with the individual on this path when it becomes imperative to take stock and to acknowledge the call to move from one manner of being to another. It should encourage a progressive probing of death, not mainly as an ascetic exercise but to transform one's outlook and gain a larger vision of reality.

Attention must be paid to a dual summons for this power of the Resurrection to penetrate into a person's intelligence and heart. *Externally*, events, the possibilities arising at every stage, people, and especially Jesus impel one to forge ahead. *On the inside*, the Holy Spirit imbues us with the light and the love that simultaneously humanize and divinize.

Conclusion

IN THESE PAGES I have tried to show that, short of self-delusion, we cannot halt at the level of limited fulfilment. As opposed to animal desires, human desire builds on awareness that the self is not totally self-identical—it can be more than what it is at the present moment. The immanent law of desire is an aspiration towards development that surpasses corporal increase, for it aspires to psychological, moral, and spiritual growth. It is the individual as such who wishes to grow. Desire leads individuals to encounter themselves as beings endowed with freedom and potential, constantly open to aspects of themselves that are undefined and that are to be actualized in a responsible manner.

We also saw that there are different types of desire, but that the plurality of desires does not prevent a thoughtful person from adopting a central unifying desire. This requires that the individual has grasped the meaning of her life and allowed religious hope to emerge in that life. For Jews and Christians, this hope is attached to the will of God. This hope intensifies the many legitimate desires, with their pleasures and their exhilaration, by contemplating them with gratitude as gifts from the Creator. And thus we find greatness in what is small, the extraordinary within the ordinary, eternity in ephemera, and serenity in routine affairs as well as in times of sorrow.

But this is not all. Due to its powerful dynamic, human desire never reduces to needs to be met or a shortfall to be made up. When we truly renounce fulfilment by this or that possession, by this or that activity, or even by this or that person, we encounter a total void that leads to a plenitude. What happens here is a decisive experience, a resurrection, a liberation of desire, after which a person is no longer the same as before.

In its true desirability, mature desire discovers the unbelievable richness of relationship with the other and with God. It serenely combines profound joy with unending dissatisfaction; radical detachment and equanimity are both possible because it makes everything relative. It recognizes its finitude within an infinite horizon. Those who accept human imperfection in this sense are ready for negotiation—sometimes easy, sometimes laborious—with others, who are not there solely to respond to all of the former's expectations. Such a person patiently endures the trying asymmetry that arises when what is wished for is something that the other cannot or does not wish to provide.

Happiness accordingly is possible on earth, on condition that it is not sought as a mere string of pleasures, whether physical or cultural, nor in the guise of superficial enthusiasm or selfish euphoria. For those whose eyes are open to all facets of reality, including injustice, suffering, old age, and death, what true happiness constitutes is the great peace that mysteriously enters their heart. Beyond the varieties of optimism and pessimism, this happiness comes only to those who meditate, to those who take the time to penetrate to the bottom of their desire and then consecrate it in order to make it fruitful. It generates a marvellous compassion, of a Buddhist or Christian variety. Moreover, this attitude is not captive to individualism, for we have the reassuring inspiration of many others whose desire has been liberated by the radiance of the Holy Spirit.

Select Bibliography

Augustine. *Confessions.* Translated by Maria Boulding. Hyde Park, NY: New City, 1997.

Balzac, Honoré de. *Colonel Chabert.* Translated by Ellen Marriage and Clara Bell. N.p.: CreateSpace, http://www.gutenberg.org/ebooks/1954?msg=welcome_stranger.

————. "Melmoth Reconciled." Translated by Ellen Marriage. In *The Human Comedy.* N.p.: CreateSpace, http://www.gutenberg.org/files/1277/1277-h/1277-h.htm.

Barbaras, Renaud. *Le désir et la distance: Introduction à une phénoménologie de la perception.* Paris: Vrin, 1999.

Becker, Ernest. *The Denial of Death.* New York: Free Press, 1973.

Bibby, Reginald W. *Fragmented Gods: The Poverty and Potential of Religion in Canada.* Toronto: Irwin, 1987.

Cassian, John. *The Conferences.* Translated by Boniface Ramsey. New York: Paulist, 1997.

Causse, Jean-Daniel. "La défroque de l'ange." *Études théologiques et religieuses* 68 (1993) 557–71.

Cheng, François. *Le Dit de Tianyi.* Paris: Albin Michel, 1998.

————. *L'éternité n'est pas de trop.* Paris: Albin Michel, 2002

Comte-Sponville, André. *The Little Book of Atheist Spirituality.* Translated by Nancy Houston. New York: Penguin, 2007.

————. *Traité du désespoir et de la béatitude.* Paris: Presses Universitaires de France, 2002.

Delumeau, Jean. *Le péché et la peur: La culpabilisation en Occident (XIIIe–XVIIIe siècles).* Paris: Fayard, 1983.

Dolto, Françoise. *L'Évangile au risque de la psychanalyse,* vol. 2. Paris: Seuil (Points, 145), 1977.

————. *Au jeu du désir.* Paris: Seuil, 1981

————. *La foi au risque de la psychanalyse.* Paris: Delarge, 1981.

Dostoyevsky, Fyodor. *Crime and Punishment.* Translated by Richard Pevear and Larissa Volokhonsky. New York: Knopf, 1993.

————. *Notes from Underground* and *The Double.* Translated by Ronald Wilks. London: Penguin, 2009.

Ferry, Luc. *What Is the Good Life?* Translated by Lydia G. Cochrane. Chicago: University of Chicago Press, 2005.

Freud, Sigmund. *Civilization and Its Discontents.* Edited and translated by James Strachey. New York: Norton, 1961.

Fromm, Erich. *Man for Himself.* New York: Rinehart, 1947.

Gandhi, Mahatma. *The Bhagavadgita.* Delhi: Orient paperbacks, n.d., talks given in 1926.

Garceau, Benoît. *La voie du désir.* Montreal: Médiaspaul, 1997.

Goethe, Johann Wolfgang von. *Wilhelm Meister's Apprenticeship.* Translated by Thomas Carlyle. http://www.bartleby.com/345/authors/193.html.

Granier, Jean. *Le désir du moi.* Paris: Presses Universitaires de France, 1983.

Grelot, Pierre. "La révélation du bonheur dans l'Ancien Testament." *Lumière et vie* 52 (April–May 1961) 5–35.

Jacques, Francis. *Différence et subjectivité: Anthropologie d'un point de vue relationnel.* Paris: Aubier Montaigne, 1982.

Klein, Melanie. *Envy and Gratitude and Other Works: 1944–1963.* London: Virago, 1988.

Lacan, Jacques. *The Seminar, Book VII. The Ethics of Psychoanalysis, 1959–1960.* Translated by Dennis Porter. New York: Norton, 1992.

Lacroix, Jean. *Le désir et les désirs.* Paris: Presses Universitaires de France, 1975.

Lasch, Christopher. *The Culture of Narcissism.* New York: Warner, 1979.

Leclercq, Jean, et al. *La spiritualité du Moyen Âge.* Paris: Aubier, 1961.

Léon-Dufour, Xavier, ed. *Dictionary of Biblical Theology.* Updated 2nd ed. Ijamsville, MD: Word Among Us, 1988.

Levinas, Emmanuel. *En découvrant l'existence avec Husserl et Heidegger.* Paris: Vrin, 1974.

———. *Of God Who Comes to Mind.* Translated by Bettina Bergo. Stanford: Stanford University Press, 1998.

———. *Totality and Infinity: An Essay on Exteriority.* Translated by Antonio Lingis. Dordrecht: Kluwer Academic, 1991.

Lewis, C. S., ed. *The Pilgrim's Regress: An Allegorical Apology for Christianity, Reason and Romanticism.* 3rd ed. London: Geoffrey Bles, 1956.

———. *Surprised by Joy: The Shape of My Early Life.* London: Geoffrey Bles, 1955.

Loewe, William P., and Vernon J. Gregson, eds. *Jesus Crucified and Risen: Essays in Spirituality and Theology in Honor of Sebastian Moore.* Collegeville, MN: Liturgical, 1998.

Lonergan, Bernard J. F. *Insight: A Study of Human Understanding.* Collected Works of Bernard Lonergan, vol 3. Edited by Frederick E. Crowe and Robert M. Doran. Toronto: University of Toronto Press, 1992.

Madaule, Jacques. *Dostoïevski.* Paris: Éditions Universitaires, 1956.

Mahler, Margaret S., et al. *The Psychological Birth of the Human Infant: Symbiosis and Individuation.* New York: Basic, 1975.

Maslow, Abraham H. *Religions, Values, and Peak-Experiences.* New York: Viking, 1970.

————. *Toward a Psychology of Being*. 3rd ed. New York: Wiley, 1968.

May, Rollo. *Love and Will*. New York: Norton, 1969.

McDonald, William J., ed. *New Catholic Encyclopedia*. 17 vols. New York: McGraw-Hill, 1967–1979.

Monloubou, Louis, and F. M. Du Buit, eds. *Dictionnaire biblique universel*. Paris: Desclée, 1985.

Moore, Sebastian. *The Contagion of Jesus: Doing Theology as if It Mattered*. Maryknoll, NY: Orbis, 2008.

————. *The Crucified Jesus Is No Stranger*. Minneapolis: Seabury, 1977.

————. *The Fire and the Rose Are One*. London: Darton, Longman and Todd, 1980.

————. *The Inner Loneliness*. New York: Crossroad, 1982.

————. *Jesus the Liberator of Desire*. New York: Crossroad, 1989.

————. *Let This Mind Be in You: The Quest for Identity Through Oedipus to Christ*. Minneapolis: Seabury, 1985.

Pentkovsky, Aleksei, ed. *The Pilgrim's Tale*. New York: Paulist, 1999.

Poe, Edgar Allan. *Tales of Mystery and Imagination*. London: Bruce, n.d.

Pohier, Jacques. *Au nom du Père: Recherches théologiques et psychoanalytiques*. Paris: Cerf, 1972.

Rieff, Philip. *The Triumph of the Therapeutic*. San Francisco: Harper, 1968.

Rilke, Rainer Maria. *The Notebooks of Malte Laurids Brigge*. Translated by Stephen Mitchell. New York: Random House, 1990.

Rousseau, Jean-Jacques. "Discourse on the Origin of Inequality." Translated by Donald A. Cress. In *The Basic Political Writings*. Indianapolis, IN: Hackett, 1987.

————. *Letter to Beaumont, Letters Written from the Mountain, and Related Writings*. Translated by Christopher Kelly, et al. Lebanon, NH: Dartmouth College Press, 2013.

Roy, Louis. "A Clarifying Note on *Transcendent Experiences*." *Toronto Journal of Theology* 20 (2004) 51–56.

————. *Coherent Christianity: Toward an Articulate Faith*. Eugene, OR: Wipf and Stock, 2018.

————. "The Death of Jesus: Its Universal Impact." *New Blackfriars* 83 (Nov 2002) 517–28.

————. *Mystical Consciousness: Western Perspectives and Dialogue with Japanese Thinkers*. Albany, NY: SUNY Press, 2002.

————. "Sebastian Moore's Spiritual Vision and Christological Project." *Downside Review* 136 (2018) 165–77.

————. *Self-Actualization and the Radical Gospel*. Collegeville, MN: Liturgical, 2002.

————. *Transcendent Experiences: Phenomenology and Critique*. Toronto: University of Toronto Press, 2001.

————. "Why Is the Death of Jesus Redemptive?" In *Pondering the Passion: What's at Stake for Christians and Jews*, edited by Philip A. Cunningham, 129–39. Lanham, MD: Rowman & Littlefield, 2004.

Sartre, Jean-Paul. *Being and Nothingness: An Essay in Phenomenological Ontology.* Translated by Hazel E. Barnes. New York: Washington Square, 1966.

Schutz, Roger. *Vivre l'aujourd'hui de Dieu.* Taizé: Presses de Taizé, 1962.

Selye, Hans. *Stress without Distress.* Philadelphia: Lippincott, 1974.

Soloviev, Vladimir. *Trois entretiens sur la guerre, la morale et la religion.* Translated by B. Marchadier and F. Rouleau. Paris: O.E.I.L., 1984.

Stinissen, Wilfrid. *The Gift of Spiritual Direction: On Spiritual Guidance and Care of the Soul.* Liguori, MO: Liguori, 1999.

———. *Méditation chrétienne profonde.* Paris: Cerf, 1980.

Thomas Aquinas. "Thomas Aquinas' Works in English." http://dhspriory.org/thomas/english.

Vacant, Jean Michel Alfred, et al., eds. *Dictionnaire de théologie catholique.* 15 vols. Paris: Letouzey et Ané, 1902–50.

Vergote, Antoine. *Guilt and Desire: Religious Attitudes and Their Pathological Derivatives.* Translated by M. H. Wood. New Haven, CT: Yale University Press, 1988.

———. *In Search of a Philosophical Anthropology: A Compilation of Essays.* Translated by M. S. Muldoon. Leuven: Leuven University Press, 1996.

———. *Interprétation du langage religieux.* Paris: Seuil, 1974.

———. "Plaisir, désir, bonheur." *Les quatre fleuves: Cahiers de recherche et de réflexion religieuse* 23–24 (1986) 37–47.

———. *Religion, Belief and Unbelief.* Leuven: Leuven University Press, 1997.

———. *The Religious Man: A Psychological Study of Religious Attitudes.* Translated by Marie-Bernard Said. Dayton, OH: Pflaum, 1969.

Viller, Marcel, et al., eds. *Dictionnaire de spiritualité: Ascétique et mystique. Doctrine et histoire.* 17 vols. Paris: Beauchesne, 1932–1995.

Welte, Bernhard. *Qu'est-ce que croire?* Montreal: Fides, 1984.

The Wings of Desire. Directed by Wim Wenders, West Germany–France, 1987.

Yankelovich, Daniel. *New Rules: Searching for Self-Fulfillment in a World Turned Upside Down.* New York: Random House, 1981.

Zundel, Maurice. *Morale et mystique.* Paris: Desclée de Brouwer, 1962.